TOP **10**
BERLIN

T0182360

CONTENTS

BERLIN

INTRODUCING

Berlin's TV Tower in Mitte

WELCOME TO
BERLIN

Historic, edgy, multicultural: that's Berlin. Here, you can admire world-famous art, explore thought-provoking monuments and party at some of Europe's best clubs – all in one day. Don't want to miss a thing? With Top 10 Berlin, you'll enjoy the very best the city has to offer.

Few cities can rival Berlin's cultural credentials. Boundary-pushing street art and world-renowned clubs speak to the German capital's vibrant modern spirit, while absorbing museums and weighty historic monuments offer insight into its turbulent past. And this city has been indelibly marked by history. Reckoning with the realities of the world wars and the era-defining East–West division is an essential part of any trip to Berlin. Take a deep dive into the history of Germany's Jewish community at the Jüdisches Museum, walk around the glassy

Locals lounging by the Spree

dome of the symbolic Reichstag or revel in the anarchy of the East Side Gallery (a stretch of the Berlin Wall taken over by graffiti artists). To venture even further back in time (2,000 years or so), head to Museumsinsel, where the best of Berlin's mammoth museums await.

The German capital doesn't shy away from its past, nor does it dwell on it. Berliners know how to have fun, and as any bleary-eyed reveller will tell you, this isn't a city of early-birds. Come evening, beer gardens are bustling, while iconic clubs and underground raves keep party-goers dancing until the early hours. Not here for the nightlife? There's still plenty to keep you entertained.

Berlin's food scene is one of its biggest draws, with new Michelin-starred restaurants, legendary fast-food joints and international food markets keeping foodie fans on their toes. And while this city is famed for its hedonism, there's always space to unwind. Vast parks like the Tiergarten offer an oasis amid the buzzy city, while lush green ribbons along the river teem with sunbathers in the summer.

So, where to start? With Top 10 Berlin, of course. This pocket-sized guide gets to the heart of the city with simple lists of 10, expert local knowledge and comprehensive maps, helping you turn an ordinary trip into an extraordinary one.

THE STORY OF
BERLIN

Berlin has gone through a number of significant chapters in its lifetime. It grew from a humble village to a wealthy Prussian town, and survived two world wars and four decades of division. And today? It's one of Europe's most vibrant cities. Here's the story of how it came to be.

The Growth of a City

Berlin's written history began in the early 13th century, when it was a small settlement trading in fish and timber. A little over a century later, in 1411, Friedrich von Hohenzollern became the town's special protector, inaugurating what would become a 500-year reign for the House of Hohenzollern. Despite being hit by the bubonic plague and the Thirty Years' War over the next few centuries, the city grew steadily, and by the time Fredrich Wilhelm became Elector of Brandenburg in 1640, the population had hit an all-time high. After he ratified the Edict of Potsdam, around 15,000 Protestant Huguenots fleeing religious persecution in France were welcomed to Berlin, followed by refugees from Poland, Bohemia and Salzburg.

In 1701, the city became the capital of the new Kingdom of Prussia, one of the independent kingdoms that existed in Germany. The following centuries saw many notable Prussian leaders come to the fore, but Friedrich II (1740–1786), or "Frederick the Great", arguably made the most impact. He was fearlessly dedicated to enhancing Berlin's cultural standing and encouraged merchants to move to the city.

Imperial Capital

As Berlin rapidly industrialized during the 19th century, many of its famous landmarks were built. The driving force behind this explosion of Neo-Classical architecture was Karl Friedrich Schinkel, who built the likes of the Konzerthaus. But it wasn't all grand designs. The 1862 Hobrecht Plan urbanized swathes

An illustration depicting the Thirty Years' War

**Friedrich II (Frederick the Great),
King of Prussia from 1740 to 1786**

of the city to house people from the countryside seeking work in its factories. Modernized sanitation systems, electric street lighting, public transport and telephone lines drastically improved quality of life.

At this point, Germany was still made up of kingdoms and principalities. That would all change in 1871, when the prime minister of Prussia, Otto von Bismarck, unified Germany, naming Berlin its capital and Wilhelm I, a member of the House of Hohenzollern, its Kaiser (emperor). The following decades would see Prussia's military and economic influence in Europe grow, until World War I erupted in 1914.

A New Republic

Germany's defeat in the war, the November Revolution and Kaiser Wilhelm II's abdication in 1918 signalled the end of Hohenzollern dominance. It also marked the start of the Weimar Republic, a period of cultural growth and political instability. The arts blossomed against a backdrop of hyperinflation, unemployment and unbridled hedonism. The 1920 Greater Berlin Act also expanded the city's borders and doubled its population to 3.8 million, making it the world's third largest municipality. At this time, the Bauhaus redefined design, writer Christopher Isherwood captured Berlin's pioneering queerness and figures like dancer Anita Berber symbolized its underbelly, a place of cabaret and sexual freedom.

Moments in History

1237
Berlin is founded, and thought to be named after the ruler Albrecht der Bär (Albert the Bear).

1647
Joining the Stadtschloss with the Tiergarten, Unter den Linden is built, and swiftly becomes the city's most fashionable boulevard.

1791
The Brandenburger Tor (Brandenburg Gate), one of Germany's most recognizable landmarks, is completed.

1806
Napoleon's defeat of Prussia places Berlin under French occupation for two years.

1871
The newly appointed chancellor Otto von Bismarck founds the German Empire, naming Berlin as its capital.

1897
Berlin's Scientific-Humanitarian Committee is inaugurated, becoming the world's first gay rights organization.

1939–1945
World War II wreaks destruction on Berlin, culminating in the Battle of Berlin and Hitler's demise.

1948–1949
Allied air forces deliver over two million tons (18 million tonnes) of supplies during the Berlin Airlift.

1991
In a narrow vote, Berlin beats Bonn to become the capital of a reunified Germany.

2006
A reconciliatory moment for modern Germany, the country hosts the World Cup final at Berlin's Olympiastadion.

2020
After seven years of reconstruction work, the Berliner Stadtschloss opens its doors to visitors.

World War II

Berlin was still in full swing when the world stock market tanked in 1929, which set in motion the Weimar Republic's collapse and Adolf Hitler's appointment as German chancellor in 1933. Hitler despised Berlin as a place of liberals, communists and loose morals. After he leveraged the Reichstag fire in February 1933 to purge the city of his opponents, Berlin became the nerve centre of the Nazi (National Socialist German Workers') Party when they seized control a month later.

On 9 November 1938, Kristallnacht (Night of Broken Glass), a state-sponsored pogrom designed to violently intimidate Germany's Jewish population, erupted. Thousands were arrested while synagogues, schools and shops were ransacked. Hitler's invasion of Poland in 1939 signalled the start of World War II and three years later in January 1942, the Final Solution indiscriminately condemned millions of Jews to death. By the time two million Soviet Red Army soldiers rolled into Berlin in April 1945, and with Hitler having died by suicide, Berlin was a barely recognizable heap of rubble, its residents destitute and starving.

A Divided City

Germany's defeat by the Allied forces resulted in Berlin being quartered into four sectors administered by Britain, the US, France and the Soviet Union (USSR). This put the city at the

The Reichstag in ruins following the February 1933 fire

Celebrating the fall of the Wall by the Brandenburg Gate

epicentre of the Cold War (1947–1991), an ideological conflict that pitted the US and NATO against the USSR. The birth of two opposing German states in 1949 – the Federal Republic of Germany to the west and the German Democratic Republic (GDR) in the east – divided Germany once more (Britain and France administered their respective sectors until the 1990s). This split was physically cemented when the Berlin Wall went up overnight on 13 August 1961, sealing Berlin off from the West behind the Iron Curtain and cleaving families apart for the next 28 years.

West Berlin became influenced by Western Europe and the US, politically and culturally. Despite a heavy military presence and tales of espionage, artists and intellectuals flooded in, inspired by the anarchic atmosphere. Meanwhile, East Berlin stagnated under the GDR's policies. Food shortages and mass surveillance created dystopian conditions; those who tried to flee over the border were shot at by GDR authorities.

The political changes that swept through the Eastern bloc in 1989 resulted in the fall of the Wall on 9 November, and Germany was officially reunified on 3 October 1990. In many ways, undergoing this hardship allowed Berlin to blossom into the unrestricted place it is today. Progress started slowly in the 1990s; with the former East playing economic catch up with the wealthier West, times were tight. Much of East Berlin was tumbledown and squatting wasn't uncommon, but empty warehouses set the scene for non-stop raves, with techno soundtracking a renewed taste for freedom.

A New Story

People flock to modern Berlin for this unbridled freedom as well as its world-class cultural scene. It's still a safe haven for those in need, too. In response to the 2015 European migrant crisis, then Chancellor Angela Merkel championed the welcoming culture that saw Germany receive over a million refugees. Russia's 2022 invasion of Ukraine forced many Ukranians to the city, too, and Berlin is home to one of Europe's largest Palestinian diaspora communities. While right-wing populism is on the rise, Berliners remain liberal and open-minded; in an uncertain world coloured by conflict and division, this is a place where anyone can live according to their own style.

TOP 10
EXPERIENCES

Planning the perfect trip to Berlin? Whether you're visiting for the first time or making a return trip, there are some things you simply shouldn't miss out on. To make the most of your time – and to enjoy the very best this wonderfully vibrant city has to offer – be sure to add these experiences to your list.

1 Savour some street food
Currywurst, Döner kebab, *Falafel im Brot*: Berlin's street eats are legendary, the sheer variety offering a window into the city's rich cultural make-up. Hit up an *Imbiss* (food kiosk) or time-honoured market to find the comfort food of dreams, and wash your dish down with a frothy beer.

2 Museum-hop around Museumsinsel
With a whole island of museums, Berlin means business when it comes to art and culture. A UNESCO World Heritage-listed complex of five institutions (p34), including the Altes and Neues museums, Museum Island showcases 2,000 years of world history – a day well spent.

3 Look back at World War II
You can't visit Berlin without facing its dark history, and the city doesn't shy away from the impact of World War II. Reflect on the brutal reality of life under the Nazis at the Berlin Holocaust Memorial (p93), and see the city's will to rebuild at the anti-war memorial, Kaiser-Wilhelm-Gedächtnis-Kirche (p40).

4 Climb the Reichstag dome
Berlin overflows with stunning structures, and one of the very best lies atop the parliamentary building (p24). Book in advance to climb the spiral walkway that winds around the Reichstag dome, a glass structure that offers stellar views across the city.

5 Uncover Cold War history

Memories of the Cold War still loom over the capital, having shaped it into the place of solidarity it is today. For an insight into daily life in East Germany, visit the DDR (*p96*) and Stasi museums (*p149*) before stopping by the Berlin Wall Memorial (*p85*).

6 Seek out street art

Symbolic of Berlin's free-spirited nature, street art is everywhere, and the famous East Side Gallery (*p85*) is just the start. Head to Tuefelsberg (*p66*), a former Cold War spy station that's now a huge canvas, or simply amble around Friedrichshain (*p148*).

7 Indulge in the city's famed nightlife

Europe's party capital, Berlin is home to some of the world's best techno clubs. Not up for partying at Berghain (*p150*)? Blow off steam another way at a stylish speakeasy, cabaret club or classical music venue.

8 Browse weekend flea markets

Sunday is *Ruhetag* (a day of rest) and the shops are closed, so what to do? Rummage at the flea markets that pop up on squares and along the canal. A favourite is Mauerpark Flohmarkt (*p144*), which hosts an epic karaoke session.

9 Explore Berlin's parks

Perhaps surprisingly for such an urban city, Berlin's green spaces and access to forests are one of its biggest assets. Cycle through Tempelhofer Feld (*p136*), an abandoned airport-turned-people's park, or stroll around Tiergarten (*p117*), a former royal hunting estate.

10 Cruise the Spree

Flowing through the city's heart, the River Spree is a wonderful vantage point to see Berlin in all its glory. Board a boat, order a Berliner Weisse (*p81*) and look out for the likes of the Berliner Dom and the Reichstag. It's the perfect way to bookend your trip.

ITINERARIES

Seeing Brandenburger Tor, enjoying a canal-side stroll, learning about the city's layered history: there's a lot to see and do in Berlin. With places to eat, drink or simply take in the view, these itineraries offer ways to spend 2 days and 4 days in the capital.

2 DAYS

Day 1

Morning
Where better to get acquainted with Berlin than at its most famous square, Alexanderplatz (p108)? Soak up the city skyline from the Fernsehturm observation deck here and look out for Museumsinsel, an island in the Spree where you're heading next. You could spend days exploring the five museums here, but opt for the Neues Museum (p35), where you'll see the stucco-coated limestone bust of Nefertiti. The museum's Allegretto Museum Café is the perfect pitstop for a light lunch.

Afternoon
Admire the Berliner Dom (p58), the city's largest and glitziest cathedral, as you leave Museumsinsel and begin to stroll west along shady Unter den Linden (p90). This beautiful boulevard is dotted with colossal examples of Prussian-German architecture, and at

> **TRANSPORT**
> Since the city is mostly flat, cycling is a great way to get around; bike lanes and rentals are ubiquitous, and you can even take bikes on transport with a bicycle ticket.

Reichstag

Brandenburger Tor

Unter den Linden

MITTE

Philharmonie

0 metres 750
0 yards 750

Neues Museum

Deutsches Historisches Museum

Berliner Dom

DDR Museum

Fernsehturm

Alexanderplatz ①

②

East Side Galler

FISCHER-INSEL

Day 2 route continues

East Side Gallery

0 km 1
0 miles 1

Kreuzberg

BERGMANNKIEZ

Lavanderia Vecchia

Tempelhofer Feld

The opulent Berliner Dom, located on Museumsinsel

the very start you'll find the Zeughaus, the oldest and most interesting building here. Admire the sculptures that decorate the exterior then head inside, where the Deutsches Historisches Museum (p27) lies, with over one million objects that explore Germany's past. After you've had your fill of history, continue down Unter den Linden until you reach Brandenburger Tor (p22), a symbolic gate that rulers, statesmen and demonstrators have marched through over the centuries. When the sun starts to set, make for the Reichstag (p24) and climb the dome to admire Berlin bathed in a beautiful glow. It's a quick walk south to your fancy dinner spot, Facil (p121), a two-Michelin-starred restaurant that will set up your evening of classical music at the Berliner Philharmonie (p46) – just make sure to book ahead for both.

Day 2

Morning
The Cold War is a huge chapter in Berlin's story, so dedicate your morning to learning about it. Uncover how the secret police kept a watchful eye on Berliners at the DDR Museum (p96), then jump on a bus to see the remnants of the Wall that once divided the city at the East Side Gallery (p148). Soak up the colourful artwork that has adorned it since 1990, then take a short walk south via the Oberbaumbrücke to Kreuzberg (p132), one of West Berlin's poorest districts during the Cold War and today one of its most vibrant neighbourhoods. It's home to the largest Turkish community outside of Turkey, so it's only right to fuel up with a Döner kebab here.

Afternoon
Head to the Landwehrkanal (p67) to walk off your lunch, picking up a coffee to go from one of the many cafés lining the canal. It won't be long until you're in Neukölln, a creative district that's also home to one of the few hills in Berlin; climb up and you'll reach Schillerkiez, your access point to the much-loved Tempelhofer Feld (p136). This former airport is your playground for the rest of the day: cycle a loop of the tarmac, join a skating class or chill out in the community garden. Hang around to watch the sunset with a Späti beer then wind down for the night at Lavandería Vecchia (p139), a quirky Italian restaurant set in an old laundry.

> **DRINK**
> Public drinking is legal in Berlin, and buying beers from a Späti (convenience store) to drink in a park is a local pastime. You'll find plenty of these surrounding Tempelhofer Feld, and in every district around the city.

4 DAYS

Day 1

Today begins in Berlin's bustling centre, Mitte, with a visit to the Hamburger Bahnhof *(p118)*. All shows at this railway station-turned-contemporary art gallery are temporary, but they always focus on Expressionism or Pop Art, so it's guaranteed to be a colourful morning. A quick walk away is the Museum für Naturkunde *(p102)*, where you can marvel at the world's largest dinosaur skeleton. When hunger strikes, walk north to Prenzlauer Berg, where the legendary Konnopke's Imbiss *(p144)* doles out some of the best *Currywurst* in the city. The stand is located right by the U-Bahn, so hop on and head to Friedrichshain, where you can amble through the city's oldest park, Volkspark *(p67)*, where Ludwig

A sculpture on the ornamental Märchenbrunnen fountain

Hoffman's Märchenbrunnen fountain stands, and dip into the shops around Boxhagener Platz *(p148)*. You're well positioned for experiencing Berlin's iconic nightlife (Berghain, *p150*, is here), whether you succeed in getting into one of Berlin's famed clubs or settle into a slick bar, be sure to end your night belting out some tunes at Monster Ronson's Ichiban Karaoke Bar *(p150)*.

Day 2

It's over to the west of the city this morning, with much to see at Schloss

SHOP
On Sundays in the summer, Mauerpark in Prenzlauer Berg livens up with eclectic flea market stalls, talented buskers and the much-loved Bearpit Karaoke.

> **VIEW**
> Between the Jewish Museum and Topography of Terror you'll find Checkpoint Charlie, a small hut that marks the notorious border crossing between East and West Berlin; it makes for an iconic photo op.

Charlottenburg (p42), Berlin's opulent Baroque palace. Once the home of the Hohenzollern dynasty, it features beautiful English-style gardens and two magnificent buildings (each with its own entrance and fee). Spend most of the morning exploring the enchanting grounds and treasures inside, then hop on a short bus ride to Kantstraße (p127) for lunch; this is the city's best street for Asian cuisine, so take your pick from authentic Taiwanese, Chinese or Vietnamese spots. A short walk will take you to the historic boulevard Kurfürstendamm (p38), where the poignant ruins of the Kaiser-Wilhelm-Gedächtnis-Kirche stand. Also here are some of the city's best shops and boutiques; explore Bikini Berlin's (p38) independent stores before heading into KaDeWe (p82), the largest department store in Europe. When all that shopping tires you out, enjoy dinner at KaDeWe's restaurant, the Wintergarten.

Day 3

Spend the morning uncovering the profound impact that World War II had on Berlin, starting with an informative tour at the Jüdisches Museum (p133) to learn about Germany's Jewish population. Next, head to the harrowing Topography of Terror (www.topographie.de), an exhibition that details Nazi war crimes, before visiting the poignant Holocaust-Denkmal (p93). After a heavy start to the day, get some fresh air on a stroll over to Gendarmenmarkt (p92), choosing from one of the cafés in the pretty square for a leisurely lunch. A quick U-Bahn ride takes you to Potsdamer

Platz (p30), Berlin's modern centre with impressive buildings such as Das Center am Potsdamer Platz. From here continue on to the Großer Tiergarten (p66), Berlin's largest park, to reflect on the day among picturesque meadows and leafy paths. When the sun starts to set, a pint and German-Austrian food call at the waterfront Zollpackhof (p121) beer garden.

Day 4

Pack a picnic and jump on the S-Bahn out of the city centre to reach the dense woodlands of Grunewald (p99). Stroll along peaceful paths, climb up the Cold War-era listening station of Teufelsberg (p156) for sweeping views and, if it's a warm day, cool off with a swim in Teufelsee (p67), one of Berlin's many lakes. End up at Grunewaldturm (p156), where you can unwind with a drink at the beer garden beside the tower before catching a bus back into town. See out your trip to Berlin with a cruise along the Spree (p13), looking out over the city's numerous sights, before settling in for a show at the extravagant Deutsches Theater (p72).

Landscaped flowerbeds in the vast Großer Tiergarten

TOP 10 HIGHLIGHTS

The Reichstag Dome

EXPLORE THE
HIGHLIGHTS

There are some sights in Berlin you simply shouldn't miss, and it's these attractions that make the Top 10. Discover what makes each one a must-see on the following pages.

MOABIT

KAISERIN-AUGUSTA-ALLEE

BEUSSEL-STRASSE

LEVETZOWSTR.

LESSINGSTR.

FRANKLINSTR.

Spree

ALTONAER STRASSE

SPANDAUER-DAMM

OTTO-SUHR-ALLEE

KAISER-FRIEDRICH-STR.

HANSAVIERTEL

STRASSE DES 17. JUNI

BISMARCKSTRASSE

HARDENBERGSTR.

❶ Brandenburger Tor and Pariser Platz

KANTSTRASSE

❼

❷ Reichstag

KURFÜRSTENDAMM

❻

❸ Unter den Linden

LIETZENBURGER

STRASSE

❹ Potsdamer Platz

❺ Museumsinsel

❻ Kurfürstendamm

❼ Kaiser-Wilhelm-Gedachtnis-Kirche

❽ Schloss Charlottenburg

❾ Kulturforum

❿ Jüdisches Museum Berlin

MÜKKERSTR.

MITTE

HEIDESTR.

Fritz-
Schloss-
Park

INVALIDENSTRASSE

ALT-MOABIT

LUISENSTRASSE

FRIEDRICHSTRASSE

Spree

5

Spree

2

PARISER
PLATZ

3 DEN LINDEN

1 UNTER

STRASSE DES 17. JUNI

Tiergarten

MITTE

WILHELMSTRASSE

POTSDAMER
PLATZ

LEIPZIGER STR.

9

4

KOCHSTR.

AXEL-SPRINGER-ALLEE

Landwehrkanal

POTSDAMER STRASSE

STRESEMANNSTR.

10

SCHÖENBERG

KREUZBERG

DUDENSTR.

TEMPELHOF

0 kilometres   1

0 miles   1

BRANDENBURGER TOR AND PARISER PLATZ

📍 K3 🏠 Pariser Platz 🛈 Brandenburger Tor southern gatehouse; visitberlin.de

The quintessential icon of Berlin, the Brandenburg Gate stands proudly in the middle of Pariser Platz, asserting itself against the modern embassy buildings that now surround it. Crowned by its triumphant Quadriga sculpture, the famous gate has long been a focal point in Berlin's history.

1 Brandenburger Tor

This magnificent Neo-Classical structure was built by Carl G Langhans in 1789–91 and modelled on the temple porticoes of ancient Athens. A pair of pavilions, once used by guards and customs officers, frames its powerful Doric colonnade.

TOP TIP

Visit in October, when the Festival of Lights transforms the gate into a light sculpture.

2 Quadriga

The 6-m- (20-ft-) high sculpture was created in 1793 as a symbol of peace by Johann Gottfried Schadow. The sculpture, which depicts the goddess of victory driving her four-horsed chariot, is the gate's centrepiece.

3 Hotel Adlon Kempinski Berlin

Destroyed in World War II, the city's most elegant hotel is a reconstruction of the original, which hosted celebrities such as Greta Garbo, Thomas Mann and Charlie Chaplin.

4 DZ Bank

⏰ 10am–6pm Mon–Fri

The head office of DZ Bank is located in a popular modern building designed by the American architect Frank Owen Gehry. It combines the clean lines of Prussian architecture with some daring elements inside.

5 Akademie der Künste

Built in 2000–2005 and designed by Günter Behnisch and Manfred Sabatke, the Academy of Arts incorporates, behind a vast expanse of windows, the ruins of the old art academy, which was destroyed in World War II

Brandenburger Tor dominating Pariser Platz

TRANSPORT
The 100, 200 and 300 buses pass several major city sights such as Brandenburger Tor. Buy a day ticket to hop on and off.

6 French Embassy

Architect Christian de Portzamparc completed this building in 2001 on the site of the old embassy, which was ruined in World War II. Its colonnades and windows are a homage to the original.

7 American Embassy

The last gap around Pariser Platz was finally closed in 2008. A dispute had delayed building for years: the US wanted a whole street moved for reasons of security, but had to concede the point in the end.

8 Palais am Pariser Platz

This complex by Bernhard Winking is a modern interpretation of Neo-Classical architecture. Inside there is a café, a restaurant and a souvenir shop around a shaded courtyard.

9 Eugen-Gutmann-Haus

With its clean lines, the Dresdner Bank, built in 1997 by gmp, recalls the style of the New Sobriety movement of the 1920s. In front of it is Pariser Platz's famous original street sign.

10 Haus Liebermann

Josef P Kleihues built this in 1996–8, faithfully recreating the original that stood on the same site. The house is named

A EYEWITNESS TO HISTORY

The Brandenburg Gate has borne witness to many of Berlin's important events, from various military parades to celebrations marking the birth of the Third Reich and Hitler's ascent to power. It was here, too, that the Russian flag was raised in May 1945, and on 17 June 1953 that 25 workers demonstrating for better conditions were killed.

after the artist Max Liebermann, who lived here. In 1933, watching Nazi SA troops march through the gate, he famously said: "I cannot possibly eat as much, as I would like to puke."

Clockwise from right
The Pariser Platz street sign; lobby of Hotel Adlon Kempinski Berlin; glass-roofed atrium of the DZ Bank building

REICHSTAG

⊞ K2 ⊞ Platz der Republik 1 ⊞ Dome: 8am–midnight daily (last adm: 10pm); Käfer im Reichstag: 9am–1pm & 7–11pm Thu–Sat, 9am–1pm Sun ⊞ bundestag.de

No other structure is a more potent symbol of Germany's history than the Reichstag. Berlin's official parliamentary building has survived arson, revolution and war, and a tour through its fine interior is a great way to learn about the country's modern story.

1 Plenary Hall
This is the seat of the Deutscher Bundestag, the German parliament, which has convened here since 20 April 1999.

2 Portico "Dem Deutschen Volke"
The dedication "To the German People" was designed in 1916, against the will of Wilhelm II.

3 The Dome
The Reichstag dome by Lord Norman Foster affords breathtaking views of Berlin. It is open at the top to air the building.

4 Restored Façade
Despite extensive renovations, small World War II bullet holes are still visible in the building's façade.

5 Platz der Republik
Celebrations often take place on the lawn of this square in front of the Reichstag, as in 2006, the year when Germany hosted the football World Cup.

TOP TIP

To visit the dome, register online two to three days in advance.

THE REICHSTAG FIRE

When the Reichstag went up in flames on 27 February 1933, the Dutch Communist Marinus van der Lubbe was arrested for arson. It is, however, believed that the Nazis started the fire themselves as an excuse to get the "Enabling Act" passed.

Tribute to victims at the Weiße Kreuze Memorial

6 Installation "Der Bevölkerung"

Hans Haacke's work of art "To the People" is a counterpoint to the portico inscription opposite and uses the same style of lettering.

7 Weiße Kreuze Memorial

Opposite the southern side of the Reichstag, a memorial recalls the Wall, which stood only a few steps away. The white crosses commemorate the people who died at the Wall while trying to escape to West Berlin.

8 The German Flag

The giant German flag was first raised on the occasion of the official national celebrations of German reunification on 3 October 1990.

9 Memorial by Dieter Appelt

Unveiled in 1992, the memorial in front of the Reichstag commemorates 97 Social Democratic and Communist delegates who were murdered under the Third Reich.

The magnificent glass dome of the Reichstag

10 Käfer im Reichstag

This popular luxury restaurant (p121) on the Reichstag's roof offers an excellent view of the historical centre of Unter den Linden (p26).

> **EAT**
> If a meal at the Käfer im Reichstag restaurant exceeds your budget, head to one of the stalls nearby to pick up a classic Berlin Bratwurst (sausage).

Käfer im Reichstag atop the historic Reichstag

UNTER DEN LINDEN

📍 K4

The Linden, once a royal bridle path linking the king's town residence (the Stadtschloss) and Tiergarten, became Berlin's most fashionable street in the 18th century. Today, it remains one of the city's most important arteries, lined with lime trees and impressive buildings.

The grand Staatsoper Unter den Linden

1 Staatsoper Unter den Linden

📍 K4 🏠 Unter den Linden 7 🌐 staatsoper-berlin.de

The richly ornamented State Opera House is one of Germany's most attractive. Neo-Classical in style, it was built by the Prussian architect Georg Wenzeslaus von Knobelsdorff from 1741–3 as Europe's first free-standing opera house, to plans devised by Frederick the Great (p8) himself.

2 St-Hedwigs-Kathedrale

📍 K4 🏠 Bebelplatz
🔒 For renovation until autumn 2024 🌐 hedwigs-kathedrale.de

Designed by Georg Wenzeslaus von Knobelsdorff in 1740–2 and modelled on Rome's Pantheon, this is the seat of Berlin's Catholic archdiocese. It was commissioned by Frederick the Great to appease Berlin Catholics after the conquest of Silesia.

3 Humboldt-Universität

Berlin's oldest and most highly regarded university was founded in 1810 in accordance with the ideas of Wilhelm von Humboldt. Twenty-nine Nobel Prize winners were educated here, including Albert Einstein.

> **DRINK**
> Stop for some coffee and pastries at the Café Le Pupulaire, located in the Deutsche Bank's PalaisPopulaire on Unter den Linden 5.

4 Opernpalais

The building next to the Staatsoper once served as a palace for Friedrich Wilhelm III's daughters. Today it houses a centre for contemporary arts and culture, PalaisPopulaire.

5 Neue Wache

The central German memorial for all victims of war was created in 1816–8 by Karl Friedrich Schinkel. A reproduction of Käthe Kollwitz's moving *Pietà* stands here.

6 Kronprinzen-palais

Created in 1669 as a private residence by Johann Arnold Nering, the building was remodelled in 1732–3 into a Neo-Classical palace by Philip Gerlach. After World War I it became an art museum, before the East German government housed

Stately façade of Humboldt-Universität

Artworks at the German Historical Museum

state visitors there. The German reunification agreement was signed here in August 1990. It now holds cultural events and exhibitions.

7 Statue of Frederick the Great

One of Christian Daniel Rauch's grandest works (p91), this equestrian statue shows "Old Fritz"

Statue of Frederick the Great

(13.5 m/44 ft high) in his tricorn and coronation mantle.

8 Deutsches Historisches Museum

🅚 K5 🅐 Zeughaus, Unter den Linden 2 🛇 For renovation until 2026 🕙 10am–6pm daily 🕸 dhm.de

The country's largest history museum offers an overview of more than 1,000 years of German history. Housed in the Zeughaus, it is the oldest building (p29) on Unter den Linden.

9 Russische Botschaft

The huge Russian Embassy, built in Stalinist "wedding-cake style", was the first building to be erected on Unter den Linden after World War II.

GALLERY GUIDE

The ground floor of the Deutsches Historisches Museum houses exhibits from 1918 to the present. The first floor has collections from early civilizations and the Middle Ages to the early 20th century. A pathway links the Zeughaus to the temporary shows in the exhibition hall.

10 Bebelplatz

Originally named Opernplatz, this wide open space was designed by Knobelsdorff as the focal point of his Forum Fridericianum (p91). The elegant square was created to introduce some of the splendour and glory of ancient Rome to the Prussian capital. In May 1933, it became the scene of the infamous Nazi book burning.

Deutsches Historisches Museum

1. The Dying Warriors
The 22 reliefs by Andreas Schlüter, displayed on the walls of the courtyard rather than in one of the museum's exhibitions, portray the horrors of war in an unusually immediate way.

2. Europe and Asia
This group of 18th-century Meissen porcelain figures reflects the fascinating relationship between the two continents.

3. Steam Engine
A full-sized steam engine from the year 1847 marks the entrance to the exhibition on the Industrial Revolution.

4. Clothes from the Camps
Among the exhibits here that illustrate the years under Nazi rule is the jacket of a concentration camp inmate – a chilling reminder of the Third Reich.

5. Gloria Victis
The moving allegorical figure of *Gloria Victis*, created by the famed French sculptor Marius Jean Antonin Mercié, bears witness to the death of his friend during the conclusive days of the Franco-Prussian War of 1870–71.

Portrait of Martin Luther, painted by Lucas Cranach the Elder in 1529

6. Martin Luther
Luther's portrait, by Lucas Cranach the Elder, is the focal point of exhibition rooms devoted to the Reformation and Martin Luther himself.

7. V2 Rocket
Exhibited in the section on Nazi Germany is a V2 rocket engine, displayed next to an 88-mm flak gun. The V2 missile was one of the *Wunderwaffen* ("wonder weapons") used by German troops at the end of World War II.

8. Soldiers Plundering a House
This painting by Flemish-Baroque painter Sebastian Vrancx, dating from around 1600, depicts a scene from the Wars of Religion, which tore the Netherlands apart during the 16th century.

9. Saddle
A valuable saddle, dating from the middle of the 15th century, is decorated with elaborately carved plaques made of ivory.

10. The Berlin Wall
An original section of the Berlin Wall, together with banners of a peaceful pro-unification demonstration in 1989, commemorates the fall of the Wall.

Gloria Victis
by Antonin Mercié

ZEUGHAUS UNTER DEN LINDEN

Originally the royal arsenal, the Zeughaus on Unter den Linden was built in 1706 in Baroque style according to plans by the German architect Johann Arnold Nering. It is one of the street's most impressive structures, with the building surrounding a historic central courtyard that is protected by a modern glass cupola roof. Considered especially memorable are Baroque sculptor Andreas Schlüter's figures of 22 dying warriors, which are lined up along the arcades in the courtyard. They portray vividly the horrors of war. Behind the main building stands a cone-shaped glass annexe designed by the Chinese-born architect I M Pei in 2001 for special exhibitions and temporary shows. The permanent exhibition in the main building includes a collection entitled "Images and Testimonials of German History". Highlighting the most significant periods and events in the history of the country, the displays include a surprising variety of exhibits, dating from the days of the early medieval German Empire up to 1994. Featured are the important periods of the Reformation, the Thirty Years' War, the Wars of Liberation and the failed Revolution of 1848, and, of course, the more recent and unforgettable two World Wars.

Entry of Napoleon into Berlin, 27 October 1806 (1810) by Charles Meynier

4

POTSDAMER PLATZ

📍 L2

The heart of the metropolis of Berlin beats on Potsdamer Platz. A hub of urban life in the 1920s, the square became a desolate wasteland after World War II, but was revived following the fall of the Wall. Potsdamer Platz has since become a city within the city, packed with an array of entertainment, shopping and dining options that leave visitors spoilt for choice.

1 Das Center am Potsdamer Platz

🏠 Potsdamer Platz
🌐 das-center-am-potsdamer-platz.de

Formerly known as the Sony Center, this complex was designed by Helmut Jahn. It houses both a modern work-space and commercial area offering entertainment, a food hall and dining establishments.

2 Deutsche Kinemathek

🏠 Potsdamer Str. 2
🕙 10am–6pm Wed–Mon 🌐 deutsche-kinemathek.de ♿

This museum takes visitors backstage

> **TOP TIP**
>
> The square hosts a Christmas market with snowboarding and tobogganing.

at both Babelsberg (*p162*) and Hollywood with Marlene Dietrich's costumes (*p32*) and other exhibits.

3 Weinhaus Huth

The only complete building on Potsdamer Platz to have survived

The Hall of Mirrors in Deutsche Kinemathek

The skyscrapers of Potsdamer Platz

World War II, today the restored Weinhaus houses restaurants and the excellent Daimler Contemporary, which showcases modern art.

4 LEGOLAND® Discovery Centre

Potsdamer Str. 4 ☐ 10am–7pm daily ☑ legolanddiscovery centre.de 📱

This LEGO® wonderland (p71) features brick models, a miniature Berlin, a train ride to a land of dragons and a DUPLO® Village with bigger blocks for the tots.

5 Theater am Potsdamer Platz

The theatre at Marlene Dietrich Platz seats 1,800 and hosts theatrical performances, musicals and shows. Every year in February, it transforms into a venue for the Berlinale Film Festival, the "Berlinale Palast".

6 The Playce

Opened in 2022 and previously known as Potsdamer Platz

Arkaden, this shopping mall is now a food and entertainment venue. Inside, a food market, Manifesto, offers sustainable products and street food.

7 Frederick's

Bellevuestr. 1 ☐ Hours vary, check website ☑ fredericks berlin.com

Housed in the former Grand Hotel Esplanade, this 1920s-style spot has a restaurant, two bars, a lounge and deli.

8 Boulevard der Stars

Berlin's walk of fame features stars such as Marlene Dietrich, Werner Herzog, Fritz Lang, Diane

Marlene Dietrich's star on Boulevard der Stars

Enjoying the view from the 25th floor at Kollhoff Tower

Kruger, Hans Zimmer and Romy Schneider.

9 Kollhoff Tower

Potsdamer Platz 1 ☐ 11am–7pm daily (winter: to 6pm) ☑ pan oramapunkt.de 📱

Designed by Hans Kollhoff, this building has Europe's fastest lift, which takes visitors to the 25th floor viewing deck in just 20 seconds.

10 Spielbank Berlin

Marlene-Dietrich-Platz 1 ☐ 11am–3am daily ☑ spielbank-berlin.de 📱

Roulette and Black Jack can be played, and there are gambling machines too.

> **EAT**
> The Playce is home to Europe's largest food hub, Manifesto Market, where 22 restaurants offer everything from Asian to Latin American cuisine.

Deutsche Kinemathek Exhibitions

1. Weimar Republic
The exhibits here are dedicated to the works of the legendary directors of German cinema's golden age from 1918 to 1933.

2. Marlene Dietrich
This exhibition of the film star's estate includes her film costumes, her touring luggage, film clips, posters, photographs, letters and notes.

3. Metropolis
This iconic 1927 film, directed by Fritz Lang, has an alarming vision of a futuristic urban dystopian world as its subject. Models and props from the film are on display.

4. Olympia
This exhibition reveals the technical tricks used in the Nazi propaganda film *Olympia*, a staged documentary by Leni Riefenstahl made in 1936–8 after the Berlin 1936 Olympic Games.

5. Caligari
The best-known German film of the 1920s, *The Cabinet of Dr Caligari* (1920) was a masterpiece of Expressionist filmmaking by Robert Wiene.

Marlene Dietrich's famous costume collection at the Deutsche Kinemathek

Poster of the film *The Cabinet of Dr Caligari*, directed by Robert Wiene

6. National Socialism
This exhibition has documents relating to the use of film as propaganda, everyday cinema and the industry's victims: some stars continued their career under the rule of the Nazis, others refused to cooperate or were ostracized from the outset. The life and work of Jewish actor Kurt Gerron, who was persecuted and murdered, is documented as an exemplary case.

7. Post-War Cinema
The story of films and filmmaking in East and West Germany is shown here with props and costumes of popular stars of post-war German cinema such as Hanna Schygulla, Romy Schneider, Heinz Rühmann and Mario Adorf.

8. Transatlantic
This exhibition of letters, documents, keepsakes and souvenirs retraces the careers of German film stars in Hollywood, both of the silent era and the "talkies" that followed after 1928.

9. Pioneers and Divas
The early days of cinema are featured here, as well as stars of the silent era such as Henny Porten and the Dutch actress Asta Nielsen.

10. Exile
Documents in this exhibition relate to the difficulties encountered by German filmmakers when making a new start in the US in 1933–45.

THE NEW CENTRE OF BERLIN

In the 1920s, Potsdamer Platz was Europe's busiest square, featuring the first automatic traffic lights in Berlin. During World War II this social hub was razed to the ground. Ignored for almost 50 years, the empty square shifted back into the centre of Berlin when the Wall came down. During the 1990s, it was Europe's largest building site. New skyscrapers were built, and old structures were restored – some preserved rooms of the ruined historic Grand Hotel Esplanade were even physically moved into the Sony Center. Millions of people came to follow progress from the famous Red Info Box, which was removed in 2001. Altogether, around €17 billion was invested to create the present square.

The Spielbank Berlin casino in Potsdamer Platz

Das Center am Potsdamer Platz dominating Potsdamer Platz

MUSEUMSINSEL

⚲ J5 🕐 10am–6pm Tue–Sun (to 8pm Thu) 🚫 Pergamonmuseum: partially reopening 2027 🌐 smb.museum 🔗

The UNESCO Word Heritage-listed Museumsinsel is one of Berlin's most unique landmarks: a museum district located on an island formed by the two arms of the Spree River. The world's most diverse museum complex, its five fascinating museums take visitors on a cultural journey through 2,000 years of world history.

1 Altes Museum

The first building to be completed on Museumsinsel in 1830, the intriguing Altes Museum (p61) resembles a Greek temple. Originally meant to hold paintings, it now houses the collection of Classical antiquities.

2 Bode-Museum

Located at the northern tip of Museumsinsel, the Bode-Museum is a stately structure dominated by a cupola. The building holds the impressive Sculpture Collection, the Museum of Byzantine Art and the Numismatic Collection, made up of an assortment of over 500,000 objects.

3 Ägyptisches Museum

Housed within the Neues Museum, this museum (p54) features portraits of Egyptian royals and monumental architecture.

4 James-Simon-Galerie

Named in honour of James Simon (1851–1932), a patron of the Berlin State Museums, this building was designed by David Chipperfield. The museum was completed and opened in 2019.

> **TOP TIP**
>
> Access all the island's museums by getting a Museumsinsel day pass for €24.

Bust of Nefertiti in the Altes Museum

The Alte Nationalgalerie and its lovely grounds

5 Alte Nationalgalerie

First opened in 1876, the Old National Gallery (p56) was beautifully restored in the 1990s and now holds 19th-century sculptures and paintings, including works by Max Liebermann and Johann Gottfried Schadow.

6 Neues Museum

Spectacularly revamped by British architect David Chipperfield, the building itself is as fascinating as its exhibits. As well as the Museum of Pre- and Early History, the Ägyptisches Museum is also housed here.

7 Lustgarten

This "pleasure park", with a fountain in its centre, is located in front of the Altes Museum (p61). The lawns are popular with tired visitors.

8 Berliner Dom

Easily the island's most commanding structure (p58), this Baroque-style cathedral is unusually ornate for a Protestant church. Organ concerts and services can be enjoyed in this exquisitely restored building.

> **VIEW**
> Look up at the interior of the Berliner Dom to marvel at Anton von Werner's intricate mosaics, each of which contain over half a million tiles.

9 Colonnade Courtyard

This columned courtyard between the Neues Museum and the Alte Nationalgalerie connects the museums and is an atmospheric venue for open-air concerts.

10 Pergamon-museum

Built in 1909–30, this is one of the world's most important museums (p54) of ancient art and architecture, with a vast collection of antiquities.

MISSING TREASURES

During World War II, many of the island's exhibits were hidden in bunkers. Some pieces were taken by the Red Army and remain in Moscow. The Neues Museum points out the gaps in the collection.

Striking 6th-century Ishtar Gate, Pergamonmuseum

Collection Highlights

1. Pergamon Altar
The Pergamon Altar from the eponymous Greek city (in modern Turkey) dates from 160 BCE. The altar will remain closed for renovation until 2027.

2. The Mshatta Façade
A gift from Ottoman Sultan Abdul Hamid II to Kaiser Wilhelm II, and now housed in the Pergamonmusem, this stone façade elaborately carved with arabesque and animal forms was the south face of a desert fort built in 744 CE in Mshatta, Jordan.

3. The Berlin Green Head
Little is known about this beautifully crafted ancient Egyptian statue, but experts believe it was crafted around 100–50 BCE. Held in the Neues Museum, it's made from greenshist, a rock with chemicals that give it a green tone.

4. Nefertiti's Bust
The star exhibit in the Neues Museum's Egyptian Museum is a painted limestone bust of Egyptian queen Nefertiti. It was found during excavations in Egypt in 1912, and is believed to date from 1345 BCE.

Admiring the famed bust of Nefertiti in the Neues Museum

5. The Berlin Golden Hat
Part of the Neues Museum's Museum for Prehistory and Early History, this functioning calendar was created between the 9th and 8th century BCE. It's made from a paper-thin single sheet of gold and lavishly decorated with ornaments.

6. The Princesses Group
This iconic example of Neo-Classical sculpture, depicting the Crown Princess Luise of Prussia and her sister Princess Friederike of Mecklenburg-Strelitz, greets visitors at the Alte Nationalgalerie. The life-size marble structure was crafted in 1797.

7. The Lonely Tree
Of the extensive collection of German Romanticism works held at the Alte Nationalgalerie, this 1822 oil-on-canvas painting by Caspar David Friedrich is a highlight, depicting an ancient oak standing in a romantic landscape.

8. The Praying Boy
Created in 300 BCE, this Greek bronze statue was found on the island of Rhodes in the late 1400s. It's now in the Altes Museum, and depicts a naked male with his arms raised, sculpted in a Hellenistic style.

9. The Pazzi Madonna
This early Renaissance marble relief sculpture is the work of Donatello, and is said to come from the palace of the Pazzi family in Florence. Today it's found in the Bode-Museum's Sculpture Collection.

10. The Portrait Denar of Charlemagne
Held in the Numismatic collection at the Bode-Museum is this rare silver coin, created after 800 CE. One side shows a bust of Holy Roman emperor Charlemagne wearing a laurel wreath; the other shows a church with four columns.

The Berlin Green Head, one of the masterpieces in the Neus Museum's Egyptian Museum

SAVING MUSEUMSINSEL

The island of museums is a treasury of antique architecture, but until recently it had been slowly decaying. Since 1992, however, €1.8 billion has been spent on the renovation and modernization of Museumsinsel. A master plan created by renowned architects that include David Chipperfield and O M Ungers will transform the complex into a unique museum land-scape – just as it was first conceived in the 19th century by Friedrich Wilhelm IV, when he established the "free institution for art and the sciences". Once fully completed by 2037, an "architectural promenade" will serve as a conceptual and structural link between various individual museums, except the old National Gallery. This promenade will consist of a variety of rooms, courtyards and vaults, as well as exhibition halls. The core of the complex will be the James-Simon-Galerie, a central building opened in 2019. The Pergamonmuseum, which is undergoing extensive restoration, is scheduled to partially reopen in 2027.

Clockwise from left **Visitors at the spectacular Neues Museum; the eye-catching entrance to James-Simon-Galerie**

KURFÜRSTENDAMM

📍 C5

Breathtaking architecture, elegant boutiques and a lively street artist scene around Breitscheidplatz have made this shopping boulevard, known as Ku'damm, one of Berlin's most attractive and well known. At 3.8 km (2.5 miles), it's also the city's longest avenue for strolling, and a perfect way to get a feel for Berlin's vibrant energy.

1 Breitscheidplatz

Here, in the heart of the western city, artists, Berliners and visitors swarm around J Schmettan's globe fountain, known by locals as "Wasserklops" (water meatball).

EAT

One of the area's most charming cafés is the Café Wintergarten, located in the Literaturhaus on Fasanenstraße (p130). It serves great breakfast, cake and coffee in its garden.

2 Zoo Palast

This one-of-a-kind cinema was built in 1957 for the Berlinale Film Festival. Today, it is home to seven auditoriums.

3 Traffic Turret

On the corner of Joachimstaler Straße stands an old-fashioned traffic turret or *Verkehrskanzel*, the last one in the city and now a heritage monument. A police officer sat in the raised glass cabin to control traffic lights manually from 1955 until 1962, when the signals went automatic.

4 Kaiser-Wilhelm-Gedächtnis-Kirche

While the church itself was destroyed during World War II, its tower (p40) stands in the centre of the square, serving as both a memorial and a stark reminder of the terrors of war.

5 Bikini Berlin

📍 D4 🏠 Budapester Str. 38–50 🕐 10am–8pm Mon–Sat, noon–6pm Sun
🌐 bikiniberlin.de

The Bikini-Haus building, built in 1956, was renovated to house the splendid Bikini Berlin, a hip

Clockwise from right
**Neues Kranzler Eck
shopping centre;
the last standing traffic
turret in Berlin at
Kurfürstendamm; the
famous Schaubühne
theatre in Lehniner Platz**

boutique mall that also offers great views of the nearby zoo.

6 Neues Kranzler Eck

This steel-and-glass skyscraper was built in 2000 by architect Helmut Jahn. The legendary Café Kranzler was retained as a bar in front of the office block. There is an official Berlin Tourist Info centre here.

7 Iduna-Haus

The turreted building at No 59 at the Leibnitzstraße corner is one of the few surviving bourgeois houses from the late 19th century. The ornamented Jugendstil (Art Nouveau) façade has been lavishly restored.

Kurfürstendamm, Berlin's main shopping street

8 Fasanenstraße

A small street (p125) off Ku'damm, Fasanenstraße, with its galleries, expensive shops and restaurants, is one of Charlottenburg's most elegant areas.

9 Europa-Center

🗺 D4 🏠 Tauentzienstr. 9 🌐 europa-center-berlin.de
The oldest shopping centre in West Berlin, opened in 1962, is still worth a visit. Here you will find fashion boutiques, a comedy theatre and an official Berlin Tourist Info centre.

10 Lehniner Platz

The square is home to the legendary Schaubühne theatre, built as the Universum cinema in 1928 by Erich Mendelsohn and converted in 1978.

WHEN KU'DAMM WAS NO MORE THAN A LOG ROAD

In 1542, Ku'damm was just a humble "Knüppeldamm", or log road. It served the Electors as a bridle path, linking their town residence (Stadtschloss) and their hunting lodge (Jagdschloss). It was not until 1871 that the area around the boulevard developed into a fashionable "new west end". Chancellor Otto von Bismarck had the boulevard modelled on the Champs Elysées in Paris, lined with houses, shops, hotels and restaurants.

KAISER-WILHELM-GEDÄCHTNIS-KIRCHE

⊕ D4 ⌂ Breitscheidplatz ⊙ Church: noon–6pm daily; memorial hall: noon–5pm daily ⓦ gedaechtnishirche-berlin.de 🔗

This ruined Neo-Romanesque church is one of Berlin's most haunting symbols. It was consecrated in 1895 and named Kaiser Wilhelm Memorial Church in honour of Wilhelm I. It stands as both a silent reminder of the destruction of war and a symbol of the city's determination to rebuild.

1 Tower Clock
The tower clock is based on a Classical design, with Roman numerals. At night, it is lit blue by modern light-emitting diodes to match the serene lighting inside.

TOP TIP

A special music service tahes place at 6pm every Saturday.

2 Tower Ruins
Only the church tower survived the Allied bombing raids that razed much of the city to the ground in 1943. Today 71 m (233 ft) high, the tower once rose to 113 m (370 ft). The rough hole in its roof has led to its nickname, "the Hollow Tooth".

3 New Bell Tower
The hexagonal bell tower rises 53 m (174 ft) next to the tower ruins, on the site of the old church's main nave.

4 Russian Orthodox Cross
This gift from the bishops of Volokolomsk and Yuruyev was given in memory of the victims of Nazism.

5 Mosaic of the Hohenzollerns
The vividly coloured mosaic of the Hohenzollerns (p45) adorns the vestibule of the church ruins. It depicts Emperor Wilhelm I together with Queen Luise of Prussia and her entourage.

6 Main Altar
The golden figure of Christ created by Karl Hemmeter is suspended above the main altar in the modern church. In the evening light, the

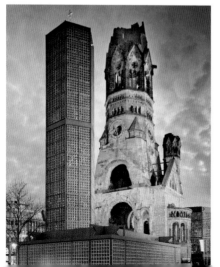

The only surviving church tower, "the Hollow Tooth"

The figure of *Christ on the Cross* above the church's altar

VIEW
Visit the church on a sunny day around lunchtime, when the blue glass window is at its most divine, with light shining through.

windows behind the altar glow an intense dark blue.

7 Kaiser's Mosaic

One of the preserved mosaics shows Heinrich I on his throne, with the imperial orb and sceptre. Originally decorated with scenes from German imperial history, the interior was intended to place the Hohenzollerns within that tradition.

8 Original Mosaics

Glittering mosaics in Jugendstil style showing Prussian dukes and princes are preserved on the walls and ceilings along the stairways.

9 Figure of Christ

Miraculously, the vast, plain sculpture of Christ, which is suspended from the ceiling, survived the bombing of the church.

10 Coventry Crucifix

This small crucifix was forged from old nails that were found in the ruins of Coventry Cathedral in England. It honours the bombing of Coventry by the German Luftwaffe in 1940.

A CHURCH WITH TWO LIVES

The Kaiser-Wilhelm-Gedächtnis-Kirche has the people of Berlin to thank for its preservation: in 1947, the Senate had planned to demolish the tower ruins for safety reasons. In a referendum, however, one in two Berliners voted to preserve it. And so the idea came about to build a new church next to the ruin and to preserve the vestibule of the old church as a striking memorial hall to the horrors of war.

Mosaic showing Kaiser Wilhelm I and the royal family

SCHLOSS CHARLOTTENBURG

📍 B3 🏠 Spandauer Damm 🌐 spsg.de ↗️

One of Berlin's premier royal sights, the former Hohenzollern summer residence offers a slice of Prussian history. The palace complex is almost a small village in itself, with its ensemble of extravagant Baroque buildings, beautifully landscaped gardens and a collection of richly decorated interiors that are unequalled in Berlin.

1 Altes Schloss
The Baroque tower of the oldest part of the palace (dating to 1695) by Johann Arnold Nering is crowned by Richard Scheibe's golden statue of Fortuna.

2 Schlosskapelle
The luxurious splendour of the palace's chapel recalls the once magnificent interior design of the complex, before it was destroyed in World War II. However, apart from the original altar, the entire chapel – including the king's box – is a costly reconstruction.

3 Neuer Flügel
Built between 1740 and 1747 by Georg W von Knobelsdorff, the New Wing contains Frederick the Great's private quarters, as well as a large collection of 18th-century French paintings.

4 Monument to the Great Elector
The equestrian statue of the Great Elector Friedrich Wilhelm is thought to be one of his most dignified portraits. Made by Andreas Schlüter

Friedrich Wilhelm

Stunning Baroque façade of Schloss Charlottenburg

between 1696 and 1703, it originally stood on the Rathausbrücke, near the destroyed Stadtschloss.

5 Käthe-Kollwitz-Museum

This museum showcases the work of sculptress and graphic artist Käthe Kollwitz (1867–1945). She was the first woman to be elected to the Prussian Academy of Arts and was later ostracized by the Nazis. Works on show include 200 drawings and prints, sculptures, a woodcut series about the war and self-portraits spanning 50 years.

6 Belvedere

Friedrich Wilhelm II liked to escape to the romantic Belvedere, a summer residence built in 1788 by Carl Gotthard Langhans, which served as a tea pavilion. Today it houses a collection of precious porcelain objects from Berlin.

7 Schlosspark

The palace has a lovely Baroque garden, beyond which lies a vast park, redesigned by Peter Joseph Lenné in 1818–28 in the English style with rivers, artificial lakes and small follies.

8 Porzellan-kabinett

This small, exquisite mirrored gallery has been faithfully restored to its original glory. Among the exhibits on display are valuable porcelain items from China and Japan.

9 Neuer Pavillon

This Italianate villa, designed by Karl Friedrich Schinkel for Friedrich Wilhelm III in 1825, was inspired by the Villa Reale del Chiatamone in Naples and clearly shows the Hohenzollerns' love of the Italian style.

10 Mausoleum

Slightly hidden, this Neo-Classical building by Schinkel is the final resting place of many Hohenzollerns.

Exquisite ceramics in the Porzellankabinett

Schloss Charlottenburg Rooms

1. Eichengalerie
The wooden panelling of the Oak Gallery is carved with expensively gilded portraits of Hohenzollern ancestors.

2. Gris-de-Lin-Kammer
This small chamber in Friedrich II's second palace apartment is decorated with paintings, including some by his favourite artist, Antoine Watteau. The room was named after its wall coverings in violet-coloured damask.

3. Schlafzimmer der Königin Luise
Queen Luise's bedchamber, designed in 1810 by Karl Friedrich Schinkel, features the clear lines typical of the Neo-Classical style.

4. Winterkammern
Friedrich Wilhelm II's early Neo-Classical rooms contain fine paintings, tapestries and furniture.

5. Grünes Zimmer
The green room in Queen Elisabeth's quarters is an excellent example of royal chambers furnished in 19th-century Biedermeier style.

6. Goldene Galerie
The festival salon in the Neuer Flügel, 42 m (138 ft) long, was designed in

The Goldene Galerie, a Rococo garden ballroom, dating from 1746

Rococo style by Frederick the Great's favourite architect, von Knobelsdorff. The richly ornamented room has a cheerful appearance.

7. Bibliothek
Frederick the Great's small but outstanding library has elegant bookcases and a vibrant, light green colour scheme.

8. Konzertkammer
The furniture and gilded panelling in the concert hall have been faithfully recreated as during Frederick the Great's time. Antoine Watteau's *Gersaint's Shop Sign*, considered to be one of his most significant works, hangs here; the king bought the work directly from the artist.

9. Rote Kammer
The elegant chamber, decorated entirely in red and gold, is adorned by portraits of King Friedrich I and Sophie Charlotte.

10. Friedrich I's Audienzkammer
The ceiling paintings and Belgian tapestries depict allegorical figures symbolizing the fine arts and the sciences. There are also magnificent lacquered cabinets, modelled on Asian originals.

Interior of the Gris-De-Lin-Kammer, a fine example of a royal chamber

THE HOHENZOLLERNS AND BERLIN

In 1411, Burggraf Friedrich of the Hohenzollern dynasty of Nuremberg was asked by Sigismund of Luxemburg to support him in a princely feuding before the imperial election for the throne. When Sigismund became king, he gave Friedrich, in 1415, the titles of Margrave and Prince-Elector of Brandenburg as a reward for his services – this is where the histories of the Hohenzollerns and Berlin first became entwined, a relationship that was to last for 500 years. From the start, the family tried to limit the powers of the town and of the Brandenburg nobility. Culture, however, flourished under the new rulers, especially the Great Elector 200 years later, who invited 20,000 Huguenot crafters to Berlin and founded an art gallery and several schools. His grandson Friedrich Wilhelm I, father of Frederick the Great, transformed the city into a military camp, with garrisons and parade grounds, and scoured it for tall men to join his guard unit. In the 19th century, however, relations between Berlin and the Hohenzollerns became decidedly less cordial.

Engraving of the Great Elector welcoming the exiled Huguenots

KULTURFORUM

L2 · West of Potsdamer Platz · smb.museum

Home to some of the most outstanding European art museums, as well as the famous concert hall of the Berlin Philharmonic Orchestra, Kulturforum attracts millions of visitors interested in culture and music. The complex, based in the former West Berlin, has been growing steadily since 1956 as a counterpoint to Museumsinsel in the former East Berlin.

structure (p62) to be built in the Kulturforum in 1960–3. Considered one of the best concert halls in the world, it is the home of the Berlin Philharmonic Orchestra. Kirill Petrenko has been conducting the orchestra since 2019.

1 Musikinstrumen-ten-Museum

Concealed behind the Philharmonie is this fascinating museum (p55) of musical instruments. More than 800 exhibits are on show here, including harpsichords and a 1929 Wurlitzer.

2 Neue Nationalgalerie

L1 · 10am–6pm Tue–Sat · smb.museum

Located in a striking steel-and-glass building designed by Mies van der Rohe, this gallery (p62) displays 20th-century art, with an emphasis on German Expressionism.

3 Philharmonie

Herbert-von-Karajan-Str. 1 · Hours vary, check website · berliner-philharmonik er.de

This tent-like building was the first new

4 Kunstgewerbe-museum

Craft objects from across Europe from the Middle Ages to the present day are on show at this museum (p54), including valuable items like the Guelph Treasure, silver from Lüneburg and Renaissance faïence.

5 Kammer-musiksaal

The smaller relative of the larger Philharmonie, this concert hall (p62) is one of Germany's most highly regarded chamber music venues.

A vintage harpsichord

TOP TIP

Free lunch concerts are held on summer Wednesdays at the Philharmonie.

Works on display at the Gemäldegalerie

6 Kupferstich-kabinett

🏠 Matthäihirchplatz 8
🕐 10am–6pm Tue–Sun

The Gallery of Prints and Drawings holds more than 550,000 prints and 110,000 drawings from many periods and countries.

7 Gemäldegalerie

🏠 Matthäihirchplatz 4/6 🕐 10am–6pm Tue–Sun (to 8pm Thu)

Berlin's largest art museum holds masterpieces of European art. They are displayed in the modern Neubau, built in 1998 by Heinz Hilmer and Christoph Sattler. The collection includes works by Bosch, Titian, and Rembrandt.

8 Kunstbibliothek

🏠 Matthäihirchplatz 6
🕐 10am–6pm Tue–Sun

The Art Library has a collection of advertising and art posters, among other items, and also hosts art and architecture exhibitions and design shows.

9 St Matthäuskirche

🏠 Matthäihirchplatz 1
🕐 11am–6pm Tue–Sun 🌐 stiftung-stmatthaeus.de ↗

This church is the only historic building preserved in the Kulturforum.

Built in 1844–6 by Stüler, it is also a venue for art installations and classical music concerts. After bomb damage in World War II, the structure was restored, making it the focal point of the Kulturforum.

10 Staats-bibliothek

Built between 1967 and 1978 by Hans Scharoun and Edgar Wisniewski, the National Library is one of the world's largest German-language libraries, with five million books, manuscripts and journals.

The distinctive glass façade of the Gemäldegalerie

Gemäldegalerie

1. Portrait of Hieronymus Holzschuher
Albrecht Dürer painted this portrait of the mayor of Nuremburg in 1529.

2. Madonna with Child and Singing Angels
A 1477 painting by Sandro Botticelli, this depicts the Madonna and Child, surrounded by angels carrying lilies.

3. The Birth of Christ
Martin Schongauer's altar painting (c 1480) is one of only a few religious paintings by the Alsatian artist that have been preserved.

4. Victorious Eros
Caravaggio's 1602 painting shows Eros, the god of love, trampling the symbols of culture, glory, science and power.

5. Portrait of the Merchant Georg Gisze
This 1532 painting by Hans Holbein, showing the Hanseatic League

Key to Floorplan
▨ Exhibition area

Gemäldegalerie Floorplan

merchant Georg Gisze counting his money, reflects the rise of the rich citizen during the Renaissance.

6. Portrait of Hendrickje Stoffels
In a 1656–7 portrait of his lover Hendrickje Stoffels, Rembrandt's focus is entirely on the subject.

7. The French Comedy
This painting by Antoine Watteau belonged to the collection of Frederick the Great.

8. The Glass of Wine
A skilfully composed scene, Vermeer's *The Glass of Wine* (1658–61) shows a couple drinking wine.

9. Venus and the Organ Player
Painted by Titian (1550–52), this piece reflects the playful sensuality typical of the Italian Renaissance.

10. Dutch Proverbs
Pieter Brueghel beautifully incorporated and literalized more than 100 proverbs into this 1559 painting.

Hans Holbein's *Portrait of the Merchant Georg Gisze*

ARCHITECTURE IN THE KULTURFORUM

The Kulturforum was planned to fill the area between Potsdamer Straße and Leipziger Platz that had been destroyed during the war. The idea for a townscape of museums and parks is credited to Berlin architect Hans Scharoun, who had designed plans for this between 1946 and 1957. It was also Scharoun who, with the building of the Philharmonie in 1963, set the character of the Kulturforum: the tent-like roofs of the music hall, the Kammermusiksaal and the National Library, designed by him and – after his death – realized by his pupil Edgar Wisniewski, are today among Berlin's top landmarks. All the buildings are characterized by the generously proportioned rooms and, although controversial when they were built, are today considered classics of modern architecture.

The tent-like roof of the Berlin Philharmonie

The Philharmonie's auditorium, known for its excellent acoustics

JÜDISCHES MUSEUM BERLIN

📍 G5 🏠 Lindenstr. 9–14 🕐 10am–7pm daily (last adm: 6pm) 🌐 jmberlin.de

The Jewish Museum is one of the most important memorials to the history and culture of Germany's Jewish community. It traces the German-Jewish relationship over the centuries. The building's symbolic design, along with the museum's important exhibits, leave a long-lasting impression. Entry is free for those under 18 years of age.

1 Libeskind Building

Designed by Daniel Libeskind, this building echoes the complex German-Jewish history – its zig-zagging floor plan, concrete "voids", and angled walls and windows sliced into the façade, are all symbolic of the Jewish experience.

2 Old Building

This Baroque building, built in 1735 as the Prussian Court of Justice, serves as the entrance to the Libeskind Building. The two buildings are connected via an underground passage. The Old Building houses the ticket counter, visitor information desk, a shop and the Eßkultur café.

3 Permanent Exhibition

The new core exhibition, "Jewish Life in Germany: Past and Present", covers, curates and explicitly presents the culture, traditions, religion and, of course, the history of the Jewish community in Germany, from the Middle Ages to the present day.

4 The Voids

A straight line of five concrete spaces, or the "voids", cut through the entire vertical axis

GALLERY GUIDE

Entrance to the main museum (the Libeshind Building) is via an underground tunnel. The exhibition is divided into 14 sections, taking visitors through German-Jewish history and culture from early history up to the present day.

The Libeskind Building housing the museum

of the Libeskind Building. These voids are intended to represent the permanent physical emptiness left behind after the Holocaust.

5 Shalekhet Installation

One of the most poignant exhibits at the museum is the *Shalekhet* (Fallen Leaves) installation by Israeli sculptor Menashe Kadishman.

It features over 10,000 iron plates, with open-mouthed faces, which visitors must walk over to cross the interesting "Memory Void" on the ground floor of the Libeskind Building.

6 Music Room

This room beautifully celebrates Jewish music and its prominent role in religious and everyday Jewish life. Immerse yourself in mellifluous chantings and soothing compositions.

7 Courtyard

The stunning glass-enclosed courtyard, part of Libeskind's design in the Old Building, and the adjoining garden provide a calm place for reflection.

8 Holocaust Tower

At the end of the Axis of the Holocaust lies the

Artworks showing Jewish life in Germany

Holocaust Tower. Designed with only one narrow slit for sunlight, the concrete tower imparts a sense of oppression and anxiety to visitors.

9 The Garden of Exile

Set on a slope, The Garden of Exile represents the disorientation and instability of life in exile. The garden is a perfect square made of 49 concrete columns, with the central column filled with earth from Jerusalem.

> **EAT**
> Café Lina, located in the Old Building, serves lunch specials that change daily, often featuring traditional Jewish and Israeli dishes as well as cakes and coffee.

10 Objects

A highlight of the museum's permanent exhibition are the objects and personal effects that narrate the history of German Jews. The collection includes art, photographs, applied art and religious artifacts.

A Hanukkah candlestick

TOP 10 OF EVERYTHING

The Holocaust Denkma

MUSEUMS

1 Pergamonmuseum
This impressive museum *(p35)* on Museumsinsel is a vast treasure trove of antiquities. It is undergoing extensive renovations and will remain closed until a partial reopening in 2027.

2 Ägyptisches Museum
📍 J5 🏛 Museumsinsel, Bodestr, 1 🕐 10am–6pm daily (to 8pm Thu) 🌐 smb.museum ♿

The star exhibit displayed at the Egyptian Museum *(p35)*, part of the Neues Museum, is the bust of Nefertiti, wife of Akhenaton. The limestone bust, excavated in 1912, was copied all over ancient Egypt. Another highlight is the Berlin Green Head, a small bust from the 4th century BCE. The museum also holds numerous mummies, sarcophagi, murals and sculptures.

3 Deutsches Historisches Museum
Germany's largest history museum *(p27)* uses unique exhibits, documents and films to take the visitor on a journey through German history, from the Middle Ages to the present day.

The modern Pei Building housing the Deutsches Historisches Museum

4 Museum Europäischer Kulturen
This museum *(p153)* specializes in European folk art, lifestyle, tradition and culture, and, with some 280,000 objects, is one of the largest of its kind in the world. It hosts long-running as well as temporary exhibitions, often in conjunction with museums from other European countries. Among the vast collection of exhibits on display are earthenware items, costumes, handicrafts, jewellery, toys and tools.

5 Kunstgewerbemuseum
📍 L1 🏛 Matthäikirchplatz 🕐 10am–6pm Tue–Fri, 11am–6pm Sat & Sun 🌐 smb.museum ♿

European crafts spanning five centuries are on display at the Museum of Decorative Arts *(p46)*. Its most valuable exhibits are the Guelph Treasure from Braunschweig and the silver treasure of the town council in Lüneburg. The museum also holds Italian tin-glazed earthenware, Renaissance faïence and German Baroque glass and ceramics. Popular displays show Neo-Classical porcelain and furniture, Jugendstil art and Tiffany vases.

6 Haus am Checkpoint Charlie
This museum *(p133)*, set at the former Allied checkpoint, hosts an exhibition documenting events at the Berlin Wall. It screens documentaries relating to the exhibition theme throughout the day. In front of the museum is the famous sign that reads, "You are now leaving the American sector," written in English, Russian, French and German.

7 Deutsches Technikmuseum
The fascinating German Museum of Technology *(p133)*, built on the site

Junkers Ju 52 plane on display at the Deutsches Technikmuseum

f a former railway goods yard,
as exciting hands-on displays
n the history of technology.

Jüdisches Museum Berlin

The Jewish Museum (p50),
oused in a spectacular building
esigned by Daniel Libeskind,
ocuments the German-Jewish
elationship through the centuries.
here are special exhibitions on
he influence of Berlin Jews on the
ity's cultural life, and on the life
f the Enlightenment philosopher
Moses Mendelssohn. An empty room
ommemorates the loss of Jewish
ulture. There is also an excellent
rogramme of special events. The
ore exhibition opened in 2020.

Museum für Naturkunde

With over 30 million intriguing
pecimens in its grand collection,
he Natural History Museum (p102)
s one of the largest of its kind in
he world. One of the star features
s the world's largest dinosaur
keleton, a Giraffatitan found in
Tanzania in 1909. There are six
more dinosaur skeletons as well
s a variety of fossils here. It is
lso worth making a visit to the
glittering exhibition of meteorites
nd minerals.

10 Musikinstrumenten-Museum

L2 ⬚Ben-Gurion-Str 1 ⬚2–7pm
Tue–Sun 🌐sim.sph-berlin.de ⬚

Some 800 musical instruments
are on display in this museum
(p46), including Frederick the
Great's harpsichord. One of the
highlights here is the silent film
organ, which still works. Saturdays
at noon is the best time to visit.

ART GALLERIES

Johannes Vermeer's *The Glass of Wine* at the Gemäldegalerie

1 Gemäldegalerie

Berlin's best art museum, the Gemäldegalerie (p47) holds European art of the 13th–19th centuries, including Vermeer's *The Glass of Wine* and *The Adoration of the Shepherds* by Hugo van der Goes, and works by Rembrandt, Dürer, Caravaggio and Rubens.

2 Alte Nationalgalerie

The Old National Gallery (p35), built by Friedrich August Stüler in 1866–76, holds a collection of 19th-century, mainly German paintings, including works by Max Liebermann, Wilhelm Leibl, Adolf von Menzel and Arnold Böcklin. It also houses sculpture by Johann Gottfried Schadow and Reinhold Begas, and is one of the many museums set on Museumsinsel (p34), an island in the Spree River.

3 Brücke-Museum

🏠 Bussardsteig 9 🕐 11am–5pm Wed–Mon 🌐 brueche-museum.de

A must-see collection of German Expressionist works by members of the artists' group Die Brücke (The Bridge), including Kirchner and Pechstein. Many Die Brücke works were labelled "degenerate" by the Nazis and destroyed.

4 Martin-Gropius-Bau

📍 F4 🏠 Niederkirchnerstr. 7 🕐 11am–7pm, Mon & Wed–Fri, 10am–7pm Sat & Sun 🌐 berlinerfestspiele.de/gropius-bau

Named after its architect Martin Gropius (1824–80), the building hosts temporary art exhibitions.

5 Kunsthaus Dahlem

📍 N6 🏠 Käuzchensteig 8 🕐 11am–5pm Wed–Mon 🌐 kunsthaus-dahlem.de

This exhibition venue for postwar German Modernism was built from

Artworks displayed at the Alte Nationalgalerie on Museumsinsel

1939–42 for sculptor Arno Breker. The building was used by US Information Control Division after the war and later became a workspace for artists.

6 C/O Berlin
⬜C4 ⬜Amerika-Haus, Hardenbergstr 22–24 ⬜11am–8pm daily ⬜co-berlin.org

Located in the former Amerika-Haus, this gallery hosts regularly changing exhibitions, lectures and historical and contemporary photography events.

7 Berlinische Galerie
⬜G5 ⬜Alte Jakobstr 124–128 ⬜10am–6pm Wed–Mon ⬜berlin ischegalerie.de

On display here are collections of German, east European and Russian painters, photographers, graphic designers and architects of the 20th century.

8 Sammlung Scharf-Gerstenberg
⬜B3 ⬜Schlossstr 70 ⬜10am–6pm Tue–Sun ⬜smb.museum

This gallery has rare works by Surrealists and their forerunners, such as Goya, Klee, Dalí, Max Ernst and Man Ray.

9 Bröhan-Museum
⬜B3 ⬜Schlossstr 1a ⬜10am–6pm Tue–Sun (free 1st Wed of month) ⬜broehan-museum.de

Jugendstil and Art Deco objects from around Europe, and paintings by Berlin artists, are on display in this museum.

10 Hamburger Bahnhof
The historic Hamburg Station (p118) houses modern artworks dating from 1960s up to the present day. The collection includes paintings, installations and multimedia art. Former dispatch warehouses were converted and linked to the old railway building, forming the Rieckhallen, and doubling the exhibition space. Among the many highlights is the Erich Marx Collection, with works by Joseph Beuys. Apart from famous artists like Andy Warhol, Jeff Koons and Robert Rauschenberg, it also showcases works by Anselm Kiefer, Sandro Chiao and others.

The Hamburger Bahnhof's impressive Neo-Classical façade and garden

CHURCHES AND SYNAGOGUES

The beautiful main altar and pulpit of the Berliner Dom

1 Berliner Dom
📍K5 ⬚Am Lustgarten ⏰Apr–Sep: 9am–8pm daily; Oct–Mar: 9am–7pm daily (opening hours subject to concert schedule, check website) 🌐berlinerdom.de ♿

Berlin Cathedral (p35), the largest and most lavish church in the city, was reopened in 1993, after almost 40 years of restoration work. Designed by Julius Raschdorf between 1894 and 1905, the building reflects the empire's aspirations to power. In particular, the black marble imperial stairs are a sign of the proximity of the Hohenzollern residence opposite the cathedral. Members of this powerful ruling dynasty are buried in the crypt. The main nave, topped by an 85-m-(279-ft-) high dome, is remarkable. The church is dominated by a splendid 20th-century Neo-Baroque pulpit and the giant Sauer organ.

2 St-Hedwigs-Kathedrale
Berlin's largest Catholic church (p26) was built by Frederick the Great in 1747–73. The cathedral is closed for renovation until late 2024.

3 Marienkirche
Work started in 1270 on the Church of St Mary (p110), which nestles at the foot of the Fernsehturm. Gothic and Baroque in style, it has an impressive Neo-Gothic tower, added in 1790 by Carl Gotthard Langhans. The font (1437) and the fresco Dance of the Dead (1485) are among the oldest treasures of the church. The richly ornamented Baroque pulpit was made by Andreas Schlüter in 1703.

4 Nikolaikirche
📍K6 ⬚Nikolaikirchplatz ⏰10am–6pm daily 🌐en.stadtmuseum.de ♿

Berlin's oldest sacred building, this church was built in 1230 in the Nikolaiviertel quarter. The present structure dates to around 1300. It is particularly famous for the portal on the west wall of the main nave, created by Andreas Schlüter. It is adorned with a gilded relief depicting a goldsmith and his wife. The church was rebuilt in 1987 and completely restored in 2009. It is now a museum exploring the history of the church and the surrounding area. Events and concerts are held here regularly.

5 Synagoge Rykestraße
The largest synagogue (p143) in Berlin, Rykestraße is one of the few Jewish places of worship in Germany to have survived Kristallnacht. It looks the same today as it did a 100 years ago.

6 Christi-Auferstehungs-Kathedrale
📍B6 ⬚Hohenzollerndamm 166 ⏰Only during services 10am & 6pm Sat, 10am Sun 🌐soborberlin.com

Berlin's largest Russian Orthodox church, the Church of Christ's Ascension

Splendid domes of the Neue Synagoge

s known for its green onion domes.
Services are held in Russian, following
Orthodox rituals.

7 Friedrichswerdersche Kirche

🏛 Werderscher Markt

This Neo-Gothic church, built
between 1824 and 1830 by Karl
Friedrich Schinkel, was originally
meant to serve the German and
French communities of the
Friedrichswerder district. Today,
the rededicated church holds the
splendid sculpture collections of
the Alte Nationalgalerie (p35).

8 Kaiser-Wilhelm-Gedächtnis-Kirche

A West Berlin landmark, this
iconic Neo-Romanesque church
(p40) successfully combines modern
architecture with the ruins of the
church tower. The church's interior
is decorated with mosaics.

9 Neue Synagoge

Once Berlin's largest synagogue,
the New Synagogue (p101) was built
originally between 1859 and 1866. It
was demolished in World War II and
partially reconstructed in 1988–95.
Its ornate dome is visible from afar.

10 Französischer Dom

📍 L4 🏛 Gendarmenmarkt 5
🕐 Summer: 10am–7pm daily;
winter: 10:30am–6:30pm daily
🌐 franzoesischer-dom.de

Standing at a height of 66 m (216 ft)
in the beautiful Gendarmenmarkt,
this elegant domed Baroque tower
(p92) dates back to between 1780 and
1789. It is a magnificent ornamental
addition to the Friedrichstadtkirche,
which was built to serve Berlin's
Huguenot community.

HISTORIC BUILDINGS

1 Reichstag
The seat of the Deutscher Bundestag, the German parliament (p24), with its spectacular dome, is a magnet for visitors.

2 Siegessäule
The Victory Column in Tiergarten (p117) is topped by a statue of the goddess Victoria. Designed by Heinrich Strack after Prussia's victory in the Danish-Prussian War of 1864, it was refurbished in 2010.

Statue of Victoria at Siegessäule

3 Rotes Rathaus
Berlin's Town Hall (p101), also known as "Red Town Hall" because of the red bricks from Brandenburg province with which it was built, harks back to the proud days when Berlin became the capital of the new Empire. Built in 1861–9 according to designs by Hermann Friedrich Waesemann, the town hall was one of Germany's largest and most magnificent buildings, built to promote the splendour of Berlin. The structure was modelled on Italian Renaissance palaces, and the tower is reminiscent of Laon cathedral in France.

4 Brandenburger Tor
More than a mere monument, the Brandenburg Gate (p22) is synonymous with Berlin. It was modelled on the entrance to the Acropolis in Athens, and has stood watch over the city since 1791.

5 Schloss Charlottenburg
Built in 1695, this palace (p42) features Baroque and Rococo splendours and a beautiful park, making it one of the most attractive in Germany. It's made up of two magnificent buildings: the Altes Schloss (Old Palace) and Neuer Flügel (New Wing).

The magnificent Reichstag topped with a modern glass dome

6 Schloss Bellevue

E3 **Spreeweg 1** **To the public** **bundespraesident.de/EN**

Built by Philipp Daniel Boumann in 1785–90, this was the residence of the Hohenzollerns until 1861. Since 1994 the stately building with its Neo-Classical façade has been the official residence of the President of the Federal Republic. The modern, egg-shaped Presidential Offices stand next to the old palace.

7 Konzerthaus

The Concert Hall is one of Karl Friedrich Schinkel's masterpieces. Built in 1818–21, it was once known as the *Schauspielhaus* (theatre), and was used as such until 1945. It was damaged during World War II, and then reopened in its new avatar as the Konzerthaus *(p92)* in 1984. The building has a portico with Ionic columns and statues of allegorical and historical personages, some riding lions and panthers, as well as deities, muses and bacchants.

8 Hackesche Höfe

This complex *(p101)* of 19th-century buildings has eight interlinked court-yards, some of which are decorated in Jugendstil style, originally by August Endell. In the early 1990s the complex was renovated. The first courtyard is particularly attractive: coloured glazed tiles with geometric patterns decorate the house from the foundations up to the guttering. In the last courtyard, trees are grouped around an idyllic well. The Hackesche Höfe is one of Berlin's most popular spots, especially on weekends, with restaurants, cafés, a cinema and the Chamäleon Theatre.

9 Altes Museum and Lustgarten

The façade of the Old Museum *(p32)*, possibly one of the most attractive Neo-Classical museum buildings in Europe, is remarkable for the 18 Ionic columns supporting a portico. Built in 1830 to Karl Friedrich Schinkel's design, it was at the time one of the first buildings to be created specifically as a museum. Originally it was to house the royal collection of paintings; today it is home to a collection of antiquities. In front of the museum is a garden *(p96)* designed by Peter Joseph Lenné. Conceived as the king's herb garden, it is now decorated with a 70-ton granite bowl by Gottlieb Christian Cantian and a fountain.

10 Zeughaus

Designed by J A Nering as the first Berlin Baroque building, the former Royal Prussian Arsenal is now the Deutsches Historisches Museum *(p27)*, with a modern addition by I M Pei.

MODERN BUILDINGS

Glitzy steel-and-glass rooftop of the Center am Potsdamer Platz

1 Das Center am Potsdamer Platz (former Sony Center)
The spectacular building complex (p30), with its unique roof, is one of Berlin's largest structures.

2 Neue Nationalgalerie
This impressive structure (p46) was constructed in 1965–8 by Mies van der Rohe. It was the first building by the pioneering Bauhaus architect after his emigration to the US. He made use of his earlier designs for the Havana headquarters of the Bacardi company, which had been abandoned after the Cuban Revolution. The collection here brings together the best of 20th-century art from Europe and North America.

3 Quartiere 205–207 Friedrichstraße
The Galeries Lafayettes and the Friedrichstadtpassagen are based within these three office blocks designed by architects Nouvel, Pei and Ungers.

4 Hauptbahnhof
🚇 J2 🚆 Hauptbahnhof
Europe's largest train station sits on the site of the historic Lehrter Bahnhof. This impressive glass-and-steel structure doubles as a retail and hospitality hub.

5 Philharmonie and Kammermusiksaal
Two modern concert halls (p46) in the Kulturforum were designed by Hans Scharoun in 1961 and 1987 respectively – the Kammermusiksaal (chamber music hall) was completed after Scharoun's death in 1972 according to his plans by his pupil Edgar Wisniewski. Both buildings are renowned for their excellent acoustics as well as for their tent-like roof structures.

Bundeskanzleramt, home of the offices of the German Chancellor

6 Bundeskanzleramt
📍 K2 🏠 Willy-Brandt-Str 1
🚪 To the public

The Chancellor's modern office complex is the only government building to have been designed by a Berlin architect. Axel Schultes developed a vast, elongated office complex, which extends north of the Reichstag, in a bend of the Spree, even stretching across the river. In the centre of the modern building stands a gleaming white cube with round windows, which Berliners quickly nicknamed the "Washing Machine". The interior of the building is decorated with valuable modern paintings. The Chancellor's office on the 7th floor has a view of the Reichstag building.

7 Nordische Botschaften
📍 D4 🏠 Rauchstr 🚪 Gallery: 10am–7pm Mon–Fri, 11am–4pm Sat & Sun 🌐 nordicembassies.org

No other embassy building has caused as much of a stir as this one housing five embassies of the Nordic countries: its green shutters open and close depending on the available light. Art exhibitions are held here regularly and there's a canteen and coffee bar.

8 Kant-Dreieck
📍 C4 🏠 Kantstr 155

The enormous "shark fin" on top of the KapHag-Group's headquarters, built by Josef Paul Kleihues in 1992–5, has become a symbol of modern Berlin. The aluminium weather vane is designed to turn in the wind like a sail. Originally, the structure, known as the "Kant Triangle", was to be built one-third higher than it is now, but the plans were vetoed by the Berlin Senate.

9 Ludwig-Erhard-Haus
📍 C4 🏠 Fasanenstr 85 🚪 8am–5pm Mon–Thu, 8am–4pm Fri 🌐 ihk.de/berlin/leh

The seat of the Berlin Stock Exchange, Ludwig-Erhard-Haus was designed by British architect Nicholas Grimshaw in 1994–8. Locals refer to it as the "armadillo" because the 15 giant metal arches of the domed building recall the animal's armour.

10 DZ Bank on Pariser Platz
This elegant building (p23) by Frank Owen Gehry combines Prussian and modern architecture. The giant dome inside is remarkable.

A free-form sculpture inside the DZ Bank building

FAMOUS BERLINERS

**Acclaimed Berlin-born actress
Marlene Dietrich**

1 Marlene Dietrich
Born in Schöneberg, Marlene Dietrich (1901–92) began her career in Berlin in the 1920s. Her breakthrough came with the film *The Blue Angel* (1931). She lies buried in the Friedenau cemetery in Steglitz. Many of her personal possessions are exhibited in the Deutsche Kinemathek *(p30)*.

2 Albert Einstein
Director of the Kaiser Wilhelm-Institute for Physics, Albert Einstein (1879–1955) was awarded the Nobel Prize for Physics in 1921. He is now better known for his Theory of Relativity, first developed in 1905. Einstein mostly lived and worked in Potsdam, but was connected with Berlin through his lectures and teaching activity. In 1933 Einstein, who was Jewish, emigrated to the US, where he stayed until his death.

3 Bertolt Brecht
Born in Augsburg, Bavaria, Bertolt Brecht (1898–1956) wrote some of his greatest works, such as the *Threepenny Opera*, in a small apartment in Charlottenburg. During the Third Reich, he emigrated to the US, and returned to Germany after the war and founded the Berliner Ensemble in East Berlin in 1949. He lived in Chausseestraße with his wife, Helene Weigel, until his death. His renovated apartment is now a museum.

4 Robert Koch
A pioneer of modern medicine, Robert Koch (1843–1910) was the Director of the Institute for Infectious Diseases. He also taught and researched at the Charité Hospital. In 1905 he received the Nobel Prize for Medicine for his discoveries in the field of tuberculosis research.

5 Käthe Kollwitz
The sculptor and painter Käthe Kollwitz (1867–1945) portrayed the social problems of the poor, and her work provides a powerful, haunting commentary on human suffering. She spent most of her life in a modest abode in the square that is now named after her, in the Prenzlauer Berg district. A monument now celebrates her works and an enlarged reproduction of her *Pietà* now adorns the Neue Wache *(p26)* war memorial.

6 Herbert von Karajan
Known as "Circus Karajani", this famous Austrian conductor (1908–1989) was head of the Berlin Philharmonic Orchestra from 1954 to 1989. During this time he helped create the orchestra's unique sound, which remains legendary to this day.

**Conductor
Herbert
von
Karajan**

Popular German poet and novelist Theodor Fontane

7 Theodor Fontane

A Huguenot, Fontane (1819–98) was one of the most influential 19th-century novelists and poets in Germany. He also worked as a journalist and critic, penning many of his articles and essays in the Café Josty on Potsdamer Platz. Fontane is particularly well known for his novel *Effi Briest* and five-volume travelogue *Wanderungen durch die Mark Brandenburg (Ramblings through the March of Brandenburg)*.

8 Jacob and Wilhelm Grimm

The brothers Jacob (1785–1863) and Wilhelm (1786–1859) Grimm are known for their classic fairy tales *Little Red Riding Hood*, *Hansel and Gretel* and *Rumpelstiltskin*. Their linguistic output was equally important. Their *German Grammar* and *German Dictionary* are standard reference works even today.

9 Georg Wilhelm Hegel

The influential philosopher Hegel (1770–1831) taught at Humboldt University from 1818 until his death. His teachings continue to inspire thinkers today.

10 Nina Hagen

Singer, songwriter and actress Nina Hagen was born in East Berlin in 1955. Known for her eccentric, theatrical style, she was at the forefront of the punk movement in the late 1970s and early 80s. She remains a beloved icon of her time.

TOP 10 INNOVATORS

1. Johann Gottfried Moritz (b 1777) **and Wilhelm Wieprecht** (b 1802)
Wieprecht and Moritz created the bass tuba and secured a patent for it in 1835.

2. Katharina (Käthe) Paulus (b 1868)
The first professional balloon pilot in Germany, Paulus won a patent for creating the first collapsable parachute in 1921.

3. Otto Lilienthal (b 1848)
A German aviation pioneer, Lilienthal made over 2,000 glider flights and started the first standard production of an aircraft.

4. Ernst Litfaß (b 1816)
Litfaß was a publisher who invented the *litfaßsäule*, a free-standing cylindrical advertising column which still bears his name today.

5. Friedrich von Hefner-Altenegk (b 1845)
While at Siemens, Hefner-Altenegk, an engineer, created a drum armature which played a huge role in the invention of the electric tram.

6. Reinhold Burger (b 1866)
In 1904 Burger patented the Thermos vacuum flask, which was a development of the work of Sir James Dewar (b 1842).

7. Oskar Picht (b 1871)
Director of a school for the visually impaired, Picht developed one of the first Braille typewriters in the world.

8. Maximilian Negwer (b 1872)
A skilled entrepreneur, Negwer invented comfortable ear protection made using wax, Vaseline and cotton wool.

9. Konrad Zuse (b 1910)
German engineer Zuse is known for creating Z1, the first programmable computer and the first real programming language, Plankalkül.

10. Herta Heuwer (b 1913)
In 1949, Heuwer created the popular German fast food dish *Currywurst* (sausage with curry sauce) at her kiosk.

PARKS AND GARDENS

1 Großer Tiergarten

The Tiergarten (p117) – the green lungs of Berlin – is the most famous park in the city. Set in the centre of town, the park covers more than 200 ha (494 acres). Originally designed in 1833–40 by Peter Joseph Lenné as a hunting estate for the Elector, in the latter half of the 19th century the park became a recreation ground for all Berliners. It attracts cyclists, joggers, sunbathers and families having picnics, especially on weekends.

2 Schlosspark Charlottenburg

🅑 B3 🏠 Schloss Charlottenburg, Spandauer Damm 🕐 Sunrise–sunset daily 🌐 spsg.de

The Palace Park is one of the most attractive and charming green spaces in Germany. Immediately behind Schloss Charlottenburg (p42) is a small but mag-nificent Baroque garden, and beyond this extends a vast park, dating back to the early 19th century. It was land-scaped in the English style and features artificial lake and river landscapes, small hidden buildings and idyllic shaded groves on the banks of ponds and streams. The park is ideal for strolling and for sunseekers.

The beautiful Schlosspark Charlottenburg in front of the palace

3 Grunewald and Teufelsberg

The Grunewald (p152), or "green forest", is the public woods in the southwest of Berlin. It is the least built-up area of woodland in the city. Parts of Grunewald are very quiet and isolated, and there are wild boar in the woods. Grunewald is also home to Teufelsberg, the Cold War-era listening tower.

4 Pfaueninsel

Peacock Island (p153), an island in the middle of Großer Wannsee that can be reached only by ferry, is a romantic spot and a leisurely getaway. In the 19th century, the island served as a love nest for King Friedrich Wilhelm II. His charming folly of a palace ruin is undergoing renovation and will be closed to the public until spring 2025. Visitors can enjoy the green spaces, which are home to dozens of peacocks.

5 Viktoriapark and Kreuzberg

The old municipal park (p134), originally designed in 1888–94 as a recreation area for local workers, is a popular sunset spot. The meadows around Kreuzberg, which rise to 30 m (98 ft), are great for sun-bathing. On top of the hill, a monument recalls the Prussian Wars of Liberation.

6 Botanischer Garten

🏠 Königin-Luise-Str. 6–8 🕐 Garden: 9am–sunset daily; museum: 10am–6pm daily 🌐 bgbm.org/en

This beautiful Botanical Garden is a paradise of flowers and plants in the southwest of the city. The vast area with 15 greenhouses was built in the late 19th century around gentle hills and picturesque ponds. The Great Palm House by Alfred Koerner has spectacular 26-m- (85-ft-) high giant bamboo from Southeast Asia. The museum introduces visitors to the world of microbiology.

Statues of fairytale characters at the fountain in Volkspark Friedrichshain

7 Volkspark Friedrichshain
📍 H2 📍 Am Friedrichshain/Friedenstrasse 🕐 24 hours daily

Berlin's oldest park (1840) is an artificial landscape of lakes and meadows and two wooded mounds, one of which is nicknamed "Mont Klamott", meaning "Mount rubble". There is also a fountain with statues of the most popular fairytale characters.

8 Tierpark Berlin
Founded in 1955, this zoo (p148) is set in the wonderful palace park of Friedrichsfelde. Within its grounds are some 860 animal species.

9 Treptower Park
The 19th-century park and garden (p148) on the banks of the Spree is famous for the Soviet Memorial, which stands next to the graves of 7,000 Red Army soldiers.

10 Britzer Schloss and Park
📍 Alt-Britz 73 🕐 Palace: 11am–6pm Tue–Sun; garden: 9am–sunset daily 🌐 schlossbritz.de

The palace in Britz, dating from 1706 and situated in a lovely park, has been meticulously refurbished with historical furniture from the Gründerzeit period after 1871.

TOP 10 LAKES, RIVERS AND CANALS

1. Spree River
📍 K1–L7 📍 Mitte, Tiergarten
Guided boat tours, romantic evening cruises and relaxing riverside walks are on offer.

2. Teufelssee, Grunewald
This is considered to be one of Berlin's cleanest and most relaxed lakes – nudists and dog lovers enjoy the peaceful banks.

3. Großer Müggelsee
Thousands congregate at Berlin's largest lake (p149) in summer to have a fun time swimming, rowing, sailing or surfing.

4. Schlachtensee
After Wannsee, this small lake is the second most popular. Avoid the crowds by going during the week.

5. Strandbad Wannsee
Europe's largest inland beach (p155) is beautifully white.

6. Lietzensee
📍 A4 📍 Kaiserdamm
Lietzensee is not suitable for swimming, but the surrounding meadows are idyllic.

7. Krumme Lanke, Fischerhüttenweg
Although many consider the lake not clean enough for bathing, it seems cleaner (but colder) than Schlachtensee.

8. Landwehrkanal
📍 C3–G5 📍 Lützowplatz
Take a boat trip along the canal to see some of Berlin's most attractive bridges, or rent a boat to explore on your own.

9. Tegeler See, Alt-Tegel
The Greenwich Promenade, from Tegeler Hafen (harbour) to Schwarzer Weg, is an attractive walk.

10. Neuer See
📍 M3 📍 Großer Tiergarten
This tranquil lake is hidden in the vast Großer Tiergarten park. On its banks is the Café am Neuen See (p119).

NOTEWORTHY NEIGHBOURHOODS

1 Kreuzberg
Like many of Berlin's neighbourhoods, Kreuzberg (*p132*) has a changing face depending on where you are. To the north lies some of the city's top attractions, such as the Jüdisches Museum (*p50*), while the east is free-spirited and multicultural, home to an underground nightlife scene and the city's best Turkish food thanks to a huge Turkish community. Then there's the west, a leafier part overlooked by grand 19th-century buildings.

2 Mitte
Meaning "middle", Mitte is Berlin's literal and metaphorical heart. Its importance cannot be overstated: it was here that Berlin was founded, and today it's home to some of its biggest attractions, from Museumsinsel (*p34*) to Potsdamer Platz (*p30*). Pockets of calm can still be found if you know where to look, like at leafy Moabit or street art hub Scheunenviertel.

3 Neukölln
Word about Berlin's coolest borough has long been out, but Neukölln (*p132*) hasn't lost its power to seduce. It's one of the city's fastest-growing districts, home to international expats and young creatives drawn in by the cheap rents, vintage stores and adult playground Tempelhofer Feld (*p136*). Though fast-gentrifying, it remains genuinely multicultural, with a strong Middle Eastern community propping up top food joints along Sonnennalle, also known as "Arab Street".

4 Schöneberg
Berlin's LGBTQ+ epicentre since the 1920s, this district (*p132*) has long attracted artists and liberals (David Bowie lived out his Berlin years here). It remains a queer stronghold today, home to welcoming bars and rainbow flags flying proudly in restaurants and bookstores. As a leafy residential neighbourhood, it also makes for wonderful strolls, with epic playgrounds that keep the kids entertained.

5 Charlottenburg
The city's most well-heeled area (*p122*) holds firmly onto the glitz and glamour of a bygone Berlin, especially along upmarket shopping boulevard Kurfürstendamm (*p38*) and the old-world Schloss Charlottenburg (*p42*). But it's not all high-end opulence, with cosy cafés and excellent Asian restaurants keeping visitors well-fed.

Catching up over a drink at one of Kreuzberg's street café terraces

6 Friedrichshain

Planning to party? Friedrichshain is the thumping centre of Berlin's clubbing scene, where a punk vibe lives strong in dive pubs and iconic clubs like Berghain (p150). It's just as cool in the daytime, with organic food shops, cute cafés and a popular flea market taking over on summer Sundays, all concentrated around Boxhagener Platz (p148).

7 Prenzlauer Berg

Before becoming the bougie place it is today, P-Berg (p140) was a bohemian hub in the 1990s. There's still edge to be found amid the leafy parks and genteel boutiques; for one, it's home to some of the city's best beer spots. Things turn up a notch on Sundays when the Mauerpark (p144) flea market hosts an epic open-air karaoke session.

8 Wedding

Not many visitors make it to Wedding, meaning there's all the more reason to visit. Slowly up-and-coming, this multicultural, working-class borough remains largely untouched by gentrification, still offering affordable eating options, eclectic architecture and plenty of green space.

Boats on the edge of Treptower Park, a lovely green space in Treptow

9 Treptow

Often overlooked by visitors heading to the central districts, this green haven in the southeast breathes calm into the hectic city. It feels more like a village than an outer borough, home to a clutch of scenic lakes and lush green spaces, making it the ideal area for a Spree-side walk or picnic.

10 Grunewald

A quick S-Bahn ride to the west lies the sprawling Grunewald (p152), dense woodlands with forest trails and the cooling lake Teufelsee. In true Berlin style, you'll find epic street art even here, with graffiti taking over the former Cold War listening station of Teufelsberg (p156). In short, it makes for a perfect day out from the centre.

FAMILY ATTRACTIONS

1 Museum für Naturkunde
Berlin's museum of natural history *(p102)* has the biggest dinosaur skeleton on show anywhere in the world. The collections here are well presented.

2 Deutsches Technikmuseum
The technology museum *(p133)* is a giant playground, excellent for learning through play. There are locomotives to clamber over, windmills to play with and the Science Center Spectrum, where older children can conduct their own physics and technology experiments.

3 Filmpark Babelsberg
Exciting shoot-outs, a walk-on film set with a U-boat and a Wild West town are the film park's most popular attractions – and not just with the children. A tour of the former UFA-Film studios *(p162)* takes you behind the scenes: younger visitors can see costumes or admire the Little Sandman (Sandmännchen), a TV figure popular with children in East Germany since 1959. These studios were among the world's most prestigious when they were in operation here in Babelsberg from 1917 to 1945. Everywhere in the park are figures and props from well-known German films. A stunt show

The Dinosaur Hall at the Museum für Naturkunde

features fight scenes, car chases and pyrotechnics like those seen in *Inglourious Basterds*, *Valkyrie* and *Anonymous*, which were all shot here.

4 Labyrinth Kindermuseum
⬛ Osloer Str. 12 🕐 1–6pm Thu & Fri (from 11am Sat & Sun) 🌐 labyrinth-kindermuseum.de ↗

Berlin's lovely Museum for Children is particularly suitable for children at the preschool stage and in the early school years. Three or four themed exhibitions each year deal with subjects in a child-friendly and entertaining way – for example the "Pots and Pans Orchestra". Every exhibition is interactive, allowing kids to experiment. See website for details of special exhibitions and events.

5 Grips-Theater
🗺 D3 ⬛ Altonaer Str. 22 🕐 For performance times, check website 🌐 grips-theater.de ↗

This famous Berlin theatre for children has been showing the hit musical

Kids playing on a statue at the Filmpark

The entrance of LEGOLAND® Discovery Centre

Linie 1 since 1986. The play, which
is best suited to older children
and adolescents, uses a U-Bahn
line running from Kreuzberg to the
Ku'damm as a metaphor for life in
the big city. All shows are in German.

6 Museum der Illusionen
G3 ▣ Karl-Liebknecht-Str. 9
▣ 10am–8pm daily ▣ illuseum-
berlin.de ▣

Specially constructed rooms at this
optical illusion museum have visitors
believing they are, for example, the
size of a giant; each trick is accompanied by scientific explanations.

7 Zeiss-Großplanetarium
Artificial stars, planets and nebulae
take you to faraway galaxies under the
silvery dome of the planetarium *(p144)*.

8 Puppentheater-Museum
H6 ▣ Karl-Marx-Str. 135
▣ 2–6pm Tue–Sun ▣ puppentheater-
museum.de ▣

At this excellent Puppet Museum,
children are allowed to perform their
own puppet shows and have a go at
being puppet theatre directors.

9 Futurium
▣ Alexanderufer 2 ▣ 10am–6pm
Wed–Mon ▣ futurium.de/en
Opened in 2019, Futurium's
eye-catching modern building

on the Spree has a fantastic
educational undertaking
that explores the question: "How
do we want to live in the future?"
The intriguing and interactive
exhibition, which is divided into
three main sections – nature, man
and technology – is especially
worth a visit for those travelling
with children.

10 LEGOLAND® Discovery Centre
Apart from the exciting 4D
cinema experience and enjoyable
rides at the world's first indoor
LEGOLAND® *(p31)* there are also
hands-on activities like model-
building workshops.

PERFORMING ARTS VENUES

1 Staatsoper Unter den Linden

Both the theatre troupe and the orchestra of the venerable Berlin Opera enjoy top reputations. Founded by Frederick the Great, this opera house (p26) is the place to see the stars of the classical music scene.

2 Philharmonie

Germany's temple of classical music still presents the best performers in the world. Designed by Scharoun, the concert hall (p46) has unique acoustics, much appreciated by artists and audience alike. Concerts by the Berlin Philharmonic Orchestra are very popular and are often sold out for weeks ahead.

3 Deutsche Oper

Berlin's most modern opera house (p128) has an elegant retro design. It was built in 1961 on the site of the former Deutsches Opernhaus, which was destroyed during World War II. The controversial 88 slabs of washed-out concrete, chosen by architect Fritz Bornemann for the main façade, replaced the classic columned portico that once stood here, leading critics to describe the building as lacking artistic formation. Concerts and

opera and ballet performances are held here, along with an extensive children's programme.

4 Chamäleon-Varieté

🅾 J5 🅾 Rosenthaler 40–1, Hachesche Höfe 🅾 For performances, chech website for details 🅾 Mon 🅦 chamaeleon.com/en

Established in 2004, the small, alternative Chamäleon stage is renowned for its innovative and unique programme. Wit and ingenuity are at the forefront of shows here, which tend to be modern circus performances with a mix of music, drama and acrobatics. If you are seated in the front row, you are likely to get pulled onto the stage.

5 Bar jeder Vernunft

🅾 C5 🅾 Schaperstr. 24 (car park Freie Volhsbühne) 🅾 Box office: noon–7pm Mon–Sat, 3–7pm Sun & hols 🅦 bar-jeder-vernunft.de/en

This venue, whose name means "devoid of all reason", is a popular comedy theatre. The cabaret offers a humorous and, at times, romantic programme of songs, chansons, reviews, cabaret, slapstick and comedy, all under an amazing mirror tent dating from the 1920s. Many stars of the international and German cabaret scene can be seen regularly among the performers here, including Tim Fischer, Georgette Dee, the Pfister Sisters and Gayle Tufts, as well as older stars such as Otto Sander.

6 Deutsches Theater

Performances at the German Theatre (p104) – one of the best – include mainly classic plays in the tradition of stage and screen actor

A captivating performance by a group of dancers at the Deutsche Oper

and director Max Reinhardt who once worked here. Experimental theatre by young playwrights is performed at the DT Baracke.

7 Theater des Westens

In addition to producing its own shows, such as *La Cage aux Folles*, this theatre (p128) also hosts guest productions such as *Blue Man Group* and *Mamma Mia*.

Statue on Theater des Westens' façade

8 Friedrichstadt-Palast

🅜 J4 🏛 Friedrichstr. 107
🌐 palast.berlin/en

Shiny glass tiles and a white, plumed neon sign adorn the eyecatching façade of the Friedrichstadt-Palast, whose long-legged dancers are as popular today as they were in the 1920s. The original venue was damaged during World War II and replaced in the 1980s. Long celebrated as being among the world's best revues, the performances have become even more spirited and entertaining today.

9 Hebbel am Ufer

🅜 F5 🏛 Hallesches Ufer 32
⏰ Performances daily, chech website for details 🌐 hebbel-am-ufer.de/en

The Hebbel am Ufer has attained cult status in Berlin, thanks to its modern and varied programme of concerts, dance, music and theatre events. The best performers from around the world appear here.

10 Volksbühne

🅜 H2 🏛 Rosa-Luxemburg-Platz 🌐 volksbuehne-berlin.de

Opened in 1914 as a "theatre of the people", the iconic, avant-garde Volksbühne offers cosmopolitan theatre, dance and musical performances, and contemporary visual art.

LGBTQ+ BERLIN

Celebrating Christopher Street Day, Berlin's main LGBTQ+ Pride event

1 Christopher Street Day

Every summer, Germany's largest Pride festival, Christopher Street Day (p86), transforms Berlin into a giant street party. Thousands of people walk in a parade to celebrate the LGBTQ+ community. The parade route winds from Kurfürstendamm down the Straße des 17. Juni to Siegessäule (Victory Column). At night, the party continues in the city's many queer clubs and bars.

2 Siegessäule

W siegessaeule.de
Berlin's oldest and best-selling gay magazine is named after the Victory Column. The monthly magazine includes useful information, a round-up of what's on, small ads and interviews from the city's gay scene. It is available for free in LGBTQ+ cafés and shops.

3 Mann-o-Meter

E5 **A** Bülowstr. 106
O 5–10pm Tue–Fri, 4–8pm Sat & Sun **W** mann-o-meter.de
This is Berlin's best-known advice centre for gay and bisexual men that offers all kinds of help. Apart from psychological support relating to AIDS, safe sex and coming out, its counsellors offer help in finding accommodation, give support to those in troubled relationships and provide legal advice. Mann-o-Meter is also a good starting point for gay visitors to Berlin who wish to find out about the LGBTQ+ scene. There's also a café here.

4 SchwuZ

A Rollbergstr. 26 **O** 11pm Wed, Fri and Sat **W** schwuz.de
Located inside an ex-brewery in Neukölln, this lively queer club has been running since 1977 and is considered to be one of the best venues for parties for the LGBTQ+ community in Berlin. The vibrant parties are often themed, for which details can be found in magazines such as *Siegessäule* or on the club's Facebook page.

Artworks on the history of the LGBTQ+ community at the Schwules Museum

5 Schwules Museum
E4 **Lützowstr. 73**
2–6pm Mon, Wed–Sun
(to 8pm Thu, to 7pm Sat)
schwulesmuseum.de

Situated in Tiergarten, this small Gay Museum documents, through a variety of temporary exhibitions, the high and low points of LGBTQ+ life since the 19th century. The museum was first conceptualized in 1984. Next to the museum is an archive, a small library and a venue for cultural events.

6 Tom's Bar
D5 **Motzstr. 19** From 10pm daily tomsbar.de

One of the traditional pubs in Berlin, in the centre of the city's gay heart in Motzstraße, this popular, grungey hangout is not for those who are shy and timid – Tom's is a well-known pick-up joint. Below the (rather dark and dingy) Kneipe is a darkroom.

7 Prinz-Eisenherz-Buchhandlung
D5 **Motzstr. 23** 10am–8pm Mon–Sat prinz-eisenherz.
buchhatalog.de

Germany's first openly gay bookshop, this place now stocks the entire range of German and international publications relating to the LGBTQ+ community. Its sales assistants will track down rare or out-of-stock titles at your request. The bookshop also hosts frequent literary readings.

8 SilverFuture
H6 **Weserstr. 206**
5pm–2am daily (to 3am Fri & Sat) silverfuture.net

This queer bar welcomes a mixed crowd. It is widely known as a safe, discrimination-free space for all.

9 Stueck
H5 **Schlesische Str 16, 10997 Berlin–Kreuzberg** From 7pm Mon–Sat

Stueck is located where the famous queer bar Barbie Deinhoff once stood. The history of the bar survives in Stueck's fresh new interior. The bar continues to be popular for its two-for-one Tuesdays. Thursdays are reserved for women, trans and non-binary guests.

10 SO36
A Kreuzberg classic, this famous – and infamous – dance venue *(p138)* has been very popular for many years and attracts a mixed crowd. The Sunday night club "Café Fatal", when old German chart hits and dance tunes are played, is legendary.

LOUNGES AND CLUBS

1 House of Weekend
📍 J6 🏠 Alexanderstr. 7
🕐 From 10pm Fri & Sat, noon Sun
🌐 weekendclub.berlin

This rooftop spot in an old Soviet block, with great views of the glittering high-rises on Alexanderplatz, is a trendy and surprisingly down-to-earth house, techno and electro pop club, frequented by a young, fashionable crowd.

2 Tresor Club
📍 L7 🏠 Köpenicher Str. 70
🕐 11pm–6am Wed–Sat 🌐 tresorberlin.com

Berlin's first techno club, Tresor opened in 1991 in the vaults of the former Wertheim department store. Today, it is situated in the basement and industrial halls of a giant former power station and continues to deliver the latest in electronic music with a full programme of visiting musicians and DJ sets.

3 Kater Blau
📍 K7 🏠 Holzmarkhstrastr 25 🌐 haterblau.de

A techno club with two dance floors, Kater Blau is famous for its dance parties, which start at midnight and last until the following afternoon on

Fridays and weekends. The outdoor area overlooks the river which features *Agnes*, an anchored ship. Check website for events.

4 SilverWings Club
Housed in the former Tempelhof Airport building (p136), this 1950s US Air Force Officers Club (p138) is ideal for dances and events. It hosts legendary theme parties on Saturday nights, which draw a crowd that prefers rock 'n' roll, soul and new wave music.

5 Spin dler & Klatt
📍 L7 🏠 Köpenicher Str. 16
🕐 Restaurant: from 7pm daily; club: from 11pm Fri & Sat 🌐 spindlerhlatt.com

This event space doubles as a regular lounge with a pan-Asian restaurant, but it is famous for hosting parties.

6 Sage Club
📍 L7 🏠 Köpenicher Str. 76
🕐 From 7pm Thu; Kit Kat Club: from 11pm Sat & Sun 🌐 sage-club.de/en

Dating from 1997, this is one of the city's oldest and most successful clubs. With a stylish interior and an impressive state-of-the-art sound system, the Sage Club is a sure bet for a thrilling night out. On weekends it

the fabulous rooftop location
of House of Weekend

hosts the notorious, clothing-optional
Kit Kat Club events (check website
for event details). The club is also
known for the eccentric bands it
books and the various DJs who
spin a range of tracks on its three
different dance floors.

7 Berghain
Set inside an East-German-era
power station, Berghain (p150) is
Berlin's hottest bastion of electronic
music. Some of the world's top DJs spin
to spectacular light shows, and the
bouncers are notoriously picky, so be
prepared to wait (or not get in at all).
Hardcore partygoers spend entire
weekends here with no sleep. The
venue is due to become a temporary
art gallery. The Panorama Bar on the
top floor affords a fantastic view over
the Spree River, while the Berghain
Garden hosts events in the summer.

8 Tausend
A great alternative to techno and
house-dominated clubs, this chic bar
is hidden under the S-Bahn tracks and
has live music. It also plays soul, jazz
and pop music from the 1970s and 80s.
Tausend has an affiliated cantina (p99)
and serves excellent mixed cocktails.

Bartenders whipping up cocktails
at the Mein Haus am See

9 Mein Haus am See
A former bookshop, this club
(p106) has comfortable seating for
guests to relax. Open 24 hours, this
place is also great for a coffee during
the day. The bar and club can get
crowded on weekends. There is a mini-
mum spend of €12.90 per person until
9pm and €19.90 per person after 9pm.

10 Watergate
🏠 Falchensteinstr. 49 🕐 From
midnight Wed, Fri & Sat 🌐 water-
gate.de
Located on the Spree River with
beautiful views of the illuminated
Oberbaumbrücke, the Watergate
is one of Berlin's cutting-edge clubs,
featuring the latest in house, techno,
and drum 'n' bass styles, plus an LED
dance floor.

KNEIPEN (PUBS) AND BARS

1 Green Door

This Berlin classic *(p138)* never goes out of style. The interior of this intimate speakeasy bar is well-hidden from the outside. Green Door attracts a young urban crowd that comes here for the cocktails and to mingle at the minimalist retro-style bar as well as along the curved, green walls. There's an outdoor bell, but the door policy is pretty liberal as long as you look sober.

2 E & M Leydicke

This slightly dated bar *(p138)* is still a big hit with tourists as well as groups of students. It regularly hosts concerts and parties featuring swing, blues, jazz and rock 'n' roll bands. Try the sweetish strawberry and raspberry wines.

3 Newton Bar

To see and be seen is the name of the game at this elegant venue *(p98)*. The service here is charming, and in summer there's even a fold-down bar on the pavement outside. Heavy leather armchairs make for comfortable sitting, and the walls are adorned with enlarged photographs of nudes by Helmut Newton, after whom the bar is named. Don't miss out on the Caribbean and Latin American cocktails.

4 Beckett's Kopf

■ H1 ◘ Pappelallee 64 ◘ 8pm–3am Wed–Sat ⬤ becketts-hopf.de
One of Berlin's finest cocktail bars, Beckett's Kopf has a portrait of writer Samuel Beckett in its window. Its dark interior features heavy velvet curtains, as if to keep the secret recipe from prying eyes. The superb concoctions include the "Mother-in-Law", with fruity notes, and the "Prince of Wales", said to be a favourite indulgence of King Edward VII.

5 Weinbar Rutz

Berlin's best (but pricey) wine bar and shop is found downstairs from the award-winning Michelin-star restaurant of the same name *(p107)*. It offers over 1,000 wines, but expert staff are on hand to assist you. There's an excellent selection of food, too.

The retro décor of Berlin's Victoria Bar

6 Victoria Bar
🅟 L2 🏠 Potsdamer Str. 102
🕐 6pm–3am Mon–Thu, 6pm–4am Fri
& Sat, 6pm–2am Sun 🌐 victoriabar.de

This cosy bar, with its understated 1960s ambience, subdued lighting and sophisticated lounge music, is a great place for a relaxing drink and has become a firm favourite among the well-to-do artsy crowd. The cocktails are mixed by the renowned barman Stefan Weber.

7 Zwiebelfisch
🅟 C4 🏠 Savignyplatz 7–8
📞 (030) 312 73 63 🕐 Noon–
6am daily

A classic venue reflecting the somewhat ageing Charlottenburg scene, Zwiebelfish is where the last survivors of the 1968 student revolt generation come to reminisce. Photographs of artists, once patrons of this establishment, are hung on the walls. In summer, there are tables outdoors.

8 Café M
🅟 E5 🏠 Goltzstr. 33 📞 (030) 216 70
92 🕐 10am–late daily (from noon
Sat & Sun)

Noisy yet laid-back, the Café M Kneipe in Schöneberg is a local favourite. Little has changed since it opened more than 40 years ago.

9 Monkey Bar
🅟 D4 🏠 Budapester Str. 40
📞 (030) 120 22 12 10 🕐 Noon–
2am daily

For beer or cocktails try this popular rooftop bar offering spectacular views of the neighbouring Berlin Zoo. It also hosts regular DJ and live music events.

10 Zum Nußbaum
One of a few traditional Kneipen in the historic Nikolaiviertel quarter, the old-fashioned Zum Nußbaum (p144) is worth checking out. It serves draught beer and features a selection of flavourful traditional Berlin food.

Patrons enjoying a drink at the traditional Zum Nußbaum pub

LOCAL DISHES

1 Döner kebab
While its specific origin story is disputed, many believe that Turkish immigrants introduced Berlin to the Döner kebab in the 1970s, igniting a passion for meat shaved from a rotisserie, paired with salad and sauces in bread. It's a perfect choice for lunch or dinner, but somehow tastes even better as a late-night snack.

2 Eisbein
Not for the faint of heart, this beloved Berlin dish consists of a tender pork knuckle (cured, boiled then roasted) with crispy skin served on a bed of pea purée and sauerkraut. It's fatty and heavy, so a slathering of *senf* (mustard) can help tackle it, as can a pint of beer from the tap. A classic German restaurant like Zur letzten Instanz (*p114*) serves it up best.

3 Currywurst
Ever since Herta Heuwer started selling it at her *Imbiss* (food stand) in 1949, *Currywurst* has been a city speciality. This fast-food staple consists of grilled, sliced sausage doused in tomato sauce (often ketchup) with a sprinkling of curry powder. Get your fix at any *Imbiss* with a side of *Pommes* (chips), and be sure to ask for your sausage unpeeled, just like the locals.

4 Bratwurst
Not to be confused with *Currywurst*, *Bratwurst* is a grilled sausage served with a white bread roll and *senf* or ketchup. Cooking methods, varieties and quality of the sausage are numerous, but the long Thüringer Rostbratwürste – a unique sausage from Thuringia – is the most popular. Seek these out at dedicated *Bratwurst* (or *Currywurst*) stands, farmers' markets and traditional German restaurants.

5 Falafel
From baklava to shawarma, Middle Eastern food is hugely popular in Berlin, and a reflection of the city's large Arab communities. For most Berliners, little beats a delicious and affordable falafel snack, whether it's a *Falafel im Brot* (falafel sandwich) or a *Falafel und Hummus Teller* (falafel plate with hummus).

6 Fischbrötchen
A fish sandwich might be more closely associated with the Baltic Coast, but Berlin serves them up just as well. Fishmongers and market stands usually offer a few fish varieties – pickled, grilled or smoked – served with remoulade and onions in a crusty white bun. If you're not squeamish, try one with *matjes*, a mild pickled herring.

Layered Baumkuchen, which translates to "tree cake" or "log cake"

7 Kaffee und Kuchen

Meeting friends and family for coffee and cake is a long-standing tradition in Germany. While it's mostly a Sunday activity, there's no need to wait to indulge; whether you head to a traditional bakery or hip café, you'll find top brews served with delicious cakes, like Baumkuchen spit cake or Käsekuchen, a German cheesecake.

8 Königsberger Klopse

Ever-present on East Prussian dinner tables, this traditional German dish shows no signs of falling out of favour, even in modern Berlin. It's the creamy caper sauce poured over the boiled meatballs that has Berliners obsessed, and a traditional inn like Max und Moritz *(p138)* is the place to try it.

9 Seasonal produce

Eating produce in season borders on an obsession in Berlin, and restaurants follow suit, celebrating whatever is ripe for picking with gusto. Expect menus to change according to the season, where a local dish might centre around *Spargel* (white and green asparagus) in spring and *Pfifferlinge* (chanterelle mushrooms) in autumn.

10 Vegan food

Berlin has long been celebrated as the vegan capital of Europe, with entire menus dedicated to meat-free fare. Whether grabbing a doughnut or tucking into a Michelin-starred meal, veganism is second nature here.

Currywurst **served with a side of fries and falafel**

TOP 10 BERLIN DRINKS

1. Berliner Weisse mit Schuss
This Berlin specialty consists of a sour wheat beer mixed with raspberry cordial or woodruff syrup, resulting in a bright red or green colour.

2. Club-Mate
Though an acquired taste, this caffeinated herbal tea-flavoured fizzy drink is perfect for a burst of energy.

3. Bier vom Fass
Germany's beers are some of the world's best, and the most highly esteemed is draught beer, enjoyed in a beer garden or *Kneipe* (pub).

4. Radler
Perfect for a summer's day, a Radler is a beer mixed with lemonade; it's often served in a half-litre bottle.

5. Späti-Bier
The lifeblood of Berlin, *Spätis* (convenience stores) offer a generous selection of half-litre bottles of beer for a couple of euros.

6. Berliner Luft
A city classic, this intense peppermint liqueur is enjoyed neat or on ice.

7. German Riesling
Wine isn't produced around Berlin, but varieties from Germany's southern and western regions have made their way here, including popular Riesling.

8. Spezi
A throwback-to-childhood drink, Spezi is a refreshing mix of orange soda and cola concocted in Germany.

9. Glühwein
Mulled wine (hot spiced red or white wine) takes over in the winter, particularly at Christmas markets.

10. Schorle
A mix of fruit juice with sparkling mineral water, Schorle comes in alcoholic and non-alcoholic varieties. *Apfelschorle* is a classic.

A refreshing jug of Schorle

SHOPS AND MARKETS

1 Art and Fashion House Quartier 206

📍 L4 🏠 Friedrichstr 71 ☎ (030) 20 94 60 00 🕐 10:30am–7:30pm Mon–Sat

This renowned shopping centre features stunning Art Deco interiors, with mosaic flooring and a marble staircase. Luxury labels such as Moschino, Etro and Bally offer stylish designer clothing and accessories,

Art Deco interior of Quartier 206, home to several luxury boutiques

while the elegant basement and first-floor cafés provide a welcome taste of Berlin coffee culture.

2 Kaufhaus des Westens (KaDeWe)

📍 D5 🏠 Tauentzienstr 21–24 ☎ (030) 212 10 🕐 10am–8pm Mon–Sat (to 9pm Fri)

Whatever you are looking for, you will find it here. Over its eight floors, the venerable Kaufhaus des Westens ("department store of the West"), affectionately called KaDeWe, offers more than three million products. On its gourmet floor, West Berlin's former "shop window", you can choose from 1,800 cheeses, 1,400 breads and pastries and 2,000 cold meats. The window displays and inner courtyards are also worth a visit in themselves.

3 Königliche Porzellan-Manufaktur (KPM)

📍 M4 🏠 Wegelystr 1 ☎ (030) 39 00 90 🕐 10am–6pm Mon–Sat

Prussia's glory and splendour to take away – traditional KPM porcelain for your dining table at home. Apart from elegant porcelain dinner services, figures and accessories made in the Berlin factory are also on sale here.

Antiques and crockery at the Antik- und Flohmarkt Straße des 17. Juni

4 Antik- und Flohmarkt Straße des 17. Juni

K1 🏠 Str des 17. Juni 🕐 10am–5pm Sat & Sun

Berlin's largest art and antiques market specializes in antique furnishings and fittings, cutlery and porcelain, books, paintings, clothing and jewellery. The traders are professionals and demand high prices, but in return you are assured of buying something truly special. With its street artists and buskers, the market is an ideal weekend spot for browsing and people-watching.

5 Mauerpark

Visiting the city's largest flea market (p144) is a Sunday pastime, not least because of the bearpit karaoke sessions held in the "bearpit" amphitheatre. Before the singing starts, browse through jewellery, vinyl records and second-hand clothes at the seemingly endless stalls.

6 Stilwerk KantGaragen

In 2022, this exclusive design and lifestyle store (p129) moved into the premises of the oldest preserved elevated garage in Europe. There are food spots and shops on the ground floor, and artwork is showcased on the spiral ramps and the upper four floors.

7 Gipsformerei Staatliche Museen

A3 🏠 Sophie-Charlotten-Str 17–18 ☎ (030) 326 76 90 🕐 9am–4pm Mon–Fri (to 6pm Wed)

If you fancy a Schinkel statue for your home or a Prussian sculpture from the Charlottenburg Palace gardens, you'll find moulded plaster reproductions here.

8 Antik- und Buchmarkt am Bode-Museum

J4 🏠 Am Kupfergraben 1 ☎ (030) 208 26 45 🕐 11am–5pm Sat & Sun

Numerous stalls offering antiques and souvenirs are scattered along the Kupfergraben in front of the Bode-Museum. Occasionally browsers can find a bargain.

9 Türkenmarkt am Maybachufer

Berlin's largest weekday Turkish market (p137) is held on Tuesdays and Fridays on the Landwehrkanal. Pick up a few picnic supplies from the market, and find a shady waterside spot to have lunch while soaking up the sun.

10 Winterfeldtmarkt

The trendiest and also the most attractive weekly food and clothing market (p137) in Berlin has developed into a hotspot with the Schöneberg crowd. On sale are a variety of high-quality goods and produce. This is the place for meeting up on Saturdays.

Potted plants and flowers at the weekly Winterfeldtmarkt

BERLIN FOR FREE

1 Schlosspark Sanssouci
For those who fancy a stroll through a Romantic landscape painting, the Schlosspark Sanssouci (p160) is a must-visit. Just a half-hour from Berlin by commuter train, these gardens in Potsdam are strewn with ponds and follies, including an Orangerie, Roman Baths modelled on an Italian villa and a Rococo-style Chinese house.

2 Reichstag
Berlin's biggest freebie happens to be a must-see attraction (p24). There's no topping the fabulous 360-degree view of the city skyline that you get from Lord Norman Foster's beautiful modern dome. Guided tours take in the plenary hall and graffiti left by Russian soldiers in 1945. Register in advance and keep your passport to enter.

3 Tempelhofer Feld
Tempelhof Flughafen was Germany's biggest airport when it was built in 1939. A powerful symbol of the new Berlin, the grounds of this historic airport were turned into an enormous public green space (p136). You will find urban gardeners, cyclists, in-line skaters, go-karters, and people barbequeing, doing Tai Chi, flying kites and playing baseball.

4 Open Monument Day
⬚ Sep ⬛ visitberlin.de
Beautiful private gardens, the interiors of historic monuments, and the hallowed halls of government ministries scattered throughout the city are opened to the public on the second Sunday in September each year. All events are free of charge.

5 Free Concerts
Churches, universities and even renowned classical orchestras give free concerts. Tickets can be booked via email (ticket@berlinerdom.de) for concerts at the lavish Berliner Dom (p58). The Berliner Philharmonica's gratis lunchtime concerts (p46), usually with small ensembles, are held every Wednesday at 1pm between September and June.

6 Free Walking Tours
⬚ Daily, year-round ⬚
Join a guided walking tour of the city run by Alternative Berlin Tours (alternativeberlin.com), Brewer's Berlin Tours (brewersberlintours.com) and New Berlin Tours (newberlintours.com). They're free of charge, although tips are encouraged, and a great way to both explore and learn about the history of the city. Check individual websites for timings and departure points.

7 Museums
Many museums and galleries, including the Alliiertenmuseum (p154), Haus der Wannsee-Konferenz (p154) and Knoblauchhaus (p110) have no admission charge. Some of Berlin's most prestigious museums,

Beautifully landscaped entrance
of Schlosspark Sanssouci

such as the Gemäldegalerie *(p47)*, the
Pergamonmuseum *(p35)* and the Alte
Nationalgalerie *(p35)* are free for
visitors under 18.

8 Holocaust-Denkmal
Designed by New York architect
Peter Eisenman, the striking Memorial
to the Murdered Jews of Europe *(p93)*
consists of 2,711 concrete pillars placed
on undulating ground. The underground Information Centre provides
a moving introduction to the horrors
that took place during the Holocaust.

9 East Side Gallery
The biggest remaining stretch *(p148)*
of the Berlin Wall is now an artistic state-
ment on Germany's division from 1961
to 1989. Famous murals include a
Trabant busting through the masonry,
Heads with Big Lips by Thierry Noir, and
Brezhnev and Honecker kissing.

**10 Gedenkstätte
Berliner Mauer**
🔲 G1 🏠 Bernauer Str. 111 🔲 Centre:
9:30am–8pm Tue–Sun 🌐 berliner-
mauer-gedenkstaette.de
The Berlin Wall Memorial is well worth
a visit for its recreated "death strip",
excellent documentary centre and
dramatic stories of how East Germans
escaped over (or under) the hated
barrier. Listening stations and displays
are spread along the former border.

Browsing the exhibits at the
Gedenkstätte Berliner Mauer

TOP 10
MONEY-SAVING TIPS

1. The city's public museums,
including the comprehensive
complex on the Museumsinsel,
are covered by the popular Berlin
Museum Pass (€29). This pass offers
free entry to all participating institutions for three consecutive days.

2. Many of Berlin's neighbourhoods
are perfect for a peaceful, leisurely
walk, and you will be surprised by
how quick and convenient it is to
travel between the city's main sights
on foot.

3. Theatres and opera houses sell
discounted tickets at the door on the
day of the performance.

4. Go gallery-hopping in the arty
Mitte district. Here, Augustrasse
and Linienstrasse teem with alluring
collections open to the public.

5. Buy a refreshing drink from a *späti*
(late-night convenience store) and
do as the locals do: sit and unwind
in one of the city's scenic parks or
by the canal for a break any time
the sun shines.

6. Buy discounted public transport
tickets (such as a four-pack or a day
pass) or hire a bicycle to get around
the city and see the lovely sites, just
like a local.

7. Bus lines 100 and 200 take in
Berlin's best sights for the price of
a single fare.

8. Take advantage of the affordable
yet delicious set menus in Berlin's
cafés and restaurants, particularly
at lunchtime.

9. Comb through the expansive
Mauerpark flea market *(p144)*, where
you can find unique vintage and
retro treasures. The market runs all
day on Sundays.

10. If you are a visitor from outside
the EU and are leaving the EU with
purchased goods, remember to get a
refund on Germany's 19 per cent sales
tax. Simply enquire with sales staff
at stores for an *Ausfuhrbescheinigung*
(export papers).

FESTIVALS AND EVENTS

1 Fashion Week
Jan & Jul ⓦ fashion-week-berlin.com/en

Top designers and local talent present their new collections at various venues throughout the city.

2 Grüne Woche
2nd half of Jan ⓦ gruene woche.de/en ⓓ

The largest gourmet feast in the world, Green Week is an agricultural and gastronomical fair for everyone. Embark on a culinary journey at the Messe Berlin exhibition grounds.

3 Internationale Tourismus Börse (ITB)
Mar ⓦ itb.com/en ⓓ

CityCube Berlin hosts the world's largest tourism fair, which offers up-to-date travel information to the general public, often at elaborately designed stalls. The nighttime shows put on by many of the exhibiting countries are especially popular.

4 Berliner Filmfestspiele
2nd & 3rd week in Feb ⓦ berlinale.de ⓓ

The Berlinale is the top German film festival, and is attended by Hollywood and German stars alike. Until 1999, the film festival took place around the Zoo-Palast cinema; today the area around Potsdamer Platz takes centre stage for the festivities.

5 Karneval der Kulturen
Whitsun (varying date in May or early Jun)

For three full days, the streets of Kreuzberg come alive with song and dance displays and street carnival parades – all celebrating Berlin's multicultural heritage.

6 Christopher Street Day
Jun & Jul ⓦ csd-berlin.de/en

A colourful Pride parade (p74) is held around the Kurfürstendamm on Christopher Street Day, in what is one of Europe's most widely attended celebrations of LGBTQ+ identity. Smaller festivities take place in other venues too, as some 500,000 people from all around the world boisterously drink and dance in the streets of Central Berlin.

7 Lange Nacht der Museen
Last weekend in Aug ⓦ lange-nacht-der-museen.de ⓓ

For one night, one ticket gives access to all the city's museums until well

Berlinale Palast
THEATER AM POTSDAMER PLATZ

Exploring the pavilions in the Internationale Funkausstellung

after midnight, offering visitors an unusual experience. Many institutions also put on special events, and street artists and sellers entertain the patiently queueing public.

8 Internationale Funkausstellung (IFA)

Early Sep ⓦ b2b.ifa-berlin.com/en ⌁
The latest in high-tech toys and entertainment technology are showcased from over 1,500 global exhibitors at the IFA (International Broadcasting Exhibition). It is held annually in the Messe Berlin exhibition grounds.

9 Pop-Kultur

End Aug/early Sep
ⓦ pop-kultur.berlin
As a successor of the Berlin Music Week, this entertaining festival for bands, musicians, artists, producers, labels and audiences is held at various venues in Kulturbrauerei in the Prenzlauer Berg district. This is a great platform to discover local musicians.

10 Festival of Lights

Oct ⓦ festival-of-lights.de
For 10 days, dozens of Berlin's modern and historical buildings are illuminated with magnificent light displays created by a number of renowned artists from across the globe.

An exciting red carpet event at the Berliner Filmfestspiele

TOP 10 SPORTS HIGHLIGHTS

1. Tempelhofer Feld
Berlin's largest sports ground
(*p136*) is a must-visit.

2. Berliner Neujahrslauf
1st Jan
A New Year's day run in the cold takes place at Brandenburger Tor.

3. Sechstagerennen
2nd half of Jan ⓦ sixday.com/en
This six-day race is one of Berlin's most popular sporting events.

4. Velocity Cycling Races
End of Jun/early Jul
ⓦ elocity.berlin
Don't miss this adrenaline-fuelled cycling race that passes through seven Berlin districts.

5. DFB-Pokalfinale
May
Germany's second-most important football cup final is played at the massive Olympiastadion.

6. Skate by Night
Jun–Aug: Sun evening
Skaters meet for nighttime "blading" at the Mercedes Benz Platz.

7. Berlin Triathlon
Early Jun ⓦ berlin-triathlon.de
Amateurs can register online for this triathlon, held every year at Treptower Park.

8. Internationales Stadionfest (ISTAF) and ISTAF Indoor
Feb and early Sep
Germany's biggest athletics festivals draw a large crowd. Events are held across the Mercedes Benz Platz and the Olympiastadion.

9. Berlin Marathon
3rd/4th Sun in Sep
ⓦ bmw-berlin-marathon.com/en
The Berlin Marathon, held at Straße des 17. Juni, attracts thousands of international runners.

10. Deutsches Traberderby
1st week in Aug
The derby for professional trotter races takes place at Trabrennbahn Mariendorf, which houses an Art Nouveau grandstand.

AREA BY AREA

Berliner Dom and the Spree River

CENTRAL BERLIN: UNTER DEN LINDEN

The boulevard of Unter den Linden is the heart of historic Mitte. Many of Berlin's historic sights are set along this significant avenue and around Bebelplatz, creating a picture of Prussian and German history from the early 18th century onwards. To the south of this avenue is the Neo-Classical Gendarmenmarkt, which is considered one of Europe's most attractive squares; the area around it is filled with elegant restaurants and cafés. Nearby is Friedrichstraße, which is lined with luxury stores and modern offices and apartments.

For places to stay in this area, see p174

1 Brandenburger Tor

Berlin's best-known landmark (p22) is located on Pariser Platz and leads through to the fashionable Unter den Linden.

2 Humboldt Forum

🅚 K5 🅐 Schloßplatz
🕐 10am–8pm Mon, Wed–Sun (to 10pm Fri & Sat) 🆆 humboldtforum.com

Designed by Franco Stella and opened in 2021, this museum and cultural complex features a rooftop terrace offering spectacular views. The exhibits on show here include artifacts from sub-Saharan Africa, Asia, Oceania and the Americas.

The magnificent Brandenburger Tor on Pariser Platz

3 Forum Fridericianum

🅚 K4 🅐 Unter den Linden and Bebelplatz

The historic structures of this complex are among the city's finest. In 1740, Frederick the Great commissioned architect von Knobelsdorff to design and construct the prestigious Neo-Classical buildings for the area around today's Bebelplatz. Frederick personally influenced their designs of Deutsche Staatsoper, Prinz-Heinrich-Palais, Alte Bibliothek and the Catholic St-Hedwigs-Kathedrale, and later the Humboldt University. The opera house was the first to be built. A memorial at Bebelplatz recalls its dark past – in 1933, it was the site of the Nazi book burning. Frederick's successors commissioned the Altes Palais and a statue of "Old Fritz", surrounded by his buildings. Christian Daniel Rauch created the bronze figure in 1840, portraying Frederick wearing his tricorn hat and coronation mantle.

FREDERICK AS ARCHITECT

Forum Fridericianum was not only Frederick the Great's memorial to himself, it also ensured that Unter den Linden became one of the greatest boulevards in Europe. The king, who favoured a Neo-Classical style, drew up plans for the buildings himself, and architect Knobelsdorff executed his ideas.

4 Museumsinsel

Museum Island (p34), a UNESCO World Heritage Site, is one of the most significant complexes of museums in the world, holding major arts collections and imposing, full-scale ancient structures across five key museums. Based here are the Pergamonmuseum (closed for renovation until 2027), the Bode-Museum, the Alte National-galerie and the Altes and Neues Museums, including the famous Ägyptisches Museum. The iconic Berliner Dom, the original Berlin Cathedral, is also located in this area.

5 Gendarmenmarkt

L4 ⬛ Mitte Konzerthaus: Gendarmenmarkt 2 ⬛ Apr–Oct: 11am–6pm ⬛ en.honzerthaus.de ⬛

This square, whose strict layout is reminiscent of an Italian Renaissance piazza, is probably the most beautiful in Berlin. Named after a regiment of *gens d'armes* stationed nearby, Gendarmenmarkt was built at the end of the 17th century as a market square. The Schauspielhaus (theatre) on the west side of the square was reopened as the Konzerthaus (concert hall) in 1984 (p61). A statue of the playwright Friedrich Schiller stands in front of the building. To the left and right of the Konzerthaus stand the twin towers of the Deutscher and Französischer doms (German and French cathedrals), dating back to the late 18th century. Französischer Dom, to its north, is a prestigious late Baroque building (p59); concealed behind it is the Französische Friedrichstadtkirche, a church serving Berlin's French community. The Deutscher Dom opposite, built in 1708 on the south side of the square for the Reformed Protestant Church, did not receive its first tower until 1785. An exhibition on democracy in Germany is on display here.

THE HUGUENOTS IN BERLIN

In 1685, the Great Elector issued the famous Edict of Potsdam, granting asylum in Berlin to around 20,000 Huguenots, who were persecuted in their native France because of their Protestant faith. Skilled academics and crafters, they moulded Berlin's social and cultural life and enriched it with the French art of living. Today, the city's French community still worships at the Friedrichstadtkirche, part of the Französischer Dom complex.

6 Friedrichstraße

J4–L4 ⬛ Mitte

Friedrichstraße has regained some of the glamour and vibrancy it possessed before World War II. Today, Berlin's Fifth Avenue is once again home to elegant shops and upmarket restaurants and cafés. Especially worth visiting are the three Quartiers 205, 206 and 207 (the latter designed by architect Jean Nouvel) within the building of Friedrichstadtpassagen and

Museumsinsel's Bode-Museum overlooking the River Spree

Art and Fashion House Quartier 206 *(p82)*. At the northern end of the street is the famous Dussmann store (books, music, events), the S-Bahn station Friedrichstraße and the former entertainment district, which includes the striking Friedrichstadt-Palast *(p73)* and the impressive Admiralspalast *(p96)*.

7 Holocaust-Denkmal
🔲 L3 🏠 Ebertstr 🕐 Information Centre: 10am–6pm Tue–Sun
🌐 stiftung-denkmal.de

The Memorial to the Murdered Jews of Europe serves as Germany's national Holocaust memorial *(p85)*. After years of debate, US star architect Peter Eisenman completed the monument in 2005. It consists of a large field with dark grey steles of varying heights up to 2 m (6 ft), which symbolize the six million Jews and others murdered by the Nazis in concentration camps between 1933 and 1945. Below the memorial, an information centre explains the causes and history of the genocide.

An eye-catching sprawl of steles at the Holocaust-Denkmal

HISTORIC MITTE WALK

Hotel Adlon Kempinski — Wilhelmstrasse — The Square
Galeries Lafayette — Borchardt
Holocaust-Denkmal — Friedrichstrasse — Gendarmenmarkt
Vossstrasse — Anton-Wilhelm-Amo Strasse
Federal Ministry of Finance

Morning
Turn back the clock on **Wilhelmstraße** *(p94)*, Berlin's political nerve centre until 1945. Starting at **Hotel Adlon Kempinski**, head south past the modern British Embassy. Turn right at Behrensstraße to visit the **Holocaust-Denkmal**, then carry on along Wilhelmstraße, where signs point out the old ministries. The Prussian State Council was in the Neo-Classical building at No 54; its last president was Konrad Adenauer, who became West Germany's first chancellor. At the corner of **Vossstraße** were Hitler's main offices in the Neue Reichskanzlei. Continue down to No 97, the giant structure of the former Ministry of Aviation. Today the **Federal Ministry of Finance** is based here. Retrace your steps north, turn right into **Anton-Wilhelm-Amo Straße** then left into **Friedrichstraße**.

Afternoon
After lunch, pop into the concept store **The Square** *(p97)* just down the street. Then head to the **Gendarmenmarkt** square nearby. Admire its Konzerthaus and the imposing Deutscher and Französischer domes. The latter holds regular classical music concerts – check their website for the schedule. Round off your day with a hearty meal at the historic **Borchardt** *(p99)* on Französische Straße.

NAZI ARCHITECTURE

One of few surviving examples of the monumental architectural style favoured by the Nazis is the former Reichsluftfahrtministerium (Ministry of Aviation), commissioned by Hermann Göring in 1935–6. The sandstone office block was the world's largest and most modern, strengthened against attack by steel girders. After reunification, the Treuhandanstalt (privatization agency) was based here; today it houses the Federal Ministry of Finance.

8 Wilhelmstraße

L3 **Between Unter den Linden and Leipziger Str.**

In imperial Berlin, the centre of the German Empire's governmental power was based in Wilhelmstraße. Around 100 years later, nothing remains of the prestigious historic buildings which represented the equivalent of No 10 Downing Street in London or Quai d'Orsay in Paris. All political decisions were made at Wilhelmstraße: both Chancellor (at No 77) and President (No 73) of the German Reich lived here in old townhouses. Their gardens became known as "ministerial gardens". Adolf Hitler had the street systematically developed into the nerve centre of Nazi power. The Neue Reichskanzlei (the Chancellor's office) was built in 1937–9 to plans by Albert Speer, at the corner of Vossstraße and Wilhelmstraße. It was blown up in 1945. Behind the Reichskanzlei was the so-called "Führerbunker" where Adolf Hitler committed suicide on 30 April 1945. It is now a car park. Of the historic buildings, only the former Ministry of Aviation (Reichsluftfahrtministerium) remains. Today, Wilhelmstraße is lined by modern residential and office buildings; the British Embassy, built in 2000 by Michael Wilford, creates a link with the international importance of this street.

9 Museum für Kommunikation

L4 **Leipziger Str. 16** **9am–5pm Tue–Fri (to 8pm Tue), 10am–6pm Sat & Sun** **mfk-berlin.de**

The world's largest Post Office Museum opened in 1872. Its excellent displays document the history of communication from the first postage stamps of the Middle Ages to today's satellite technology.

Postmodern façade of the British Embassy on Wilhelmstraße

An old European letterbox at the Museum für Kommunikation

Particularly worth seeing are a blue and a red stamp from Mauritius, one of the first telephone installations (dating back to 1863) and three talking robots who interact with the visitors. Younger visitors always enjoy the Computer-galerie, where they can learn and gain new insights while playing.

10 Schlossplatz

🗺 K5 🚇 Mitte

The Stadtschloss (town residence) of the Hohenzollerns once stood here. It was blown up by the East German government in 1950–51, and today just a few historic fragments of the original can be seen. Remains include the façade of the doorway where Karl Liebknecht is said to have proclaimed the Socialist Republic in 1918. The portal has been incorporated into the former Staatsratsgebäude (State Council Building) on the south side of the square. On its eastern side, the square used to be bordered by the Palast der Republik (Palace of the Republic), the former seat of the East German parliament demolished in 2008. The Humboldt Forum cultural centre (p91) was opened in 2021 and is set in the reconstructed Berlin Palace. It features a façade reminiscent of the old Hohenzollern Palace (p162) and a library. The non-European collections of the former Dahlem Museums (of Asian Art and of Ethnology) are housed in the building.

A DAY OF CULTURE

Morning
Start your stroll on Unter den Linden, which begins in front of the **Brandenburger Tor** on **Pariser Platz** (p22). This was Berlin's prestigious royal avenue, and the rich and famous still promenade here today. For breakfast, pop into **Einstein Unter den Linden** (p98). Afterwards continue east along the boulevard, passing the **Russian Embassy** built in 1952. From here you can already see the 13.5-m- (44-ft-) high equestrian statue of Frederick the Great at **Forum Fridericianum** (p91). This area and Bebelplatz are right in the centre of old Berlin, with the Staatsoper, Altes Palais, St-Hedwigs-Kathedrale and Humboldt-Universität around them. Stop for an early lunch at **Palais Populaire** (Unter den Linden 5) or **Café Felix at Staatsbibliothek** (Unter den Linden 8).

Afternoon
In the early afternoon continue east along Unter den Linden. At the end of the street lies the **Museumsinsel** (p34). Cross the Schloßbrücke to explore the wealth of treasures in the island's museums. If you have time, visit the **Berliner Dom** (p58). Opposite the impressive cathedral you will see **Schlossplatz**, with the **Humboldt Forum** (p91). Return along Unter den Linden to **Bocca di Bacco** (p99) or **Grill Royal** (p99) in Mitte and end your day with a delicious meal.

The Best of the Rest

1. DDR Museum

🚇 K5 🏛 Karl-Liebknecht-Str.
🕐 9am–9pm daily 🌐 ddr-museum.
de/en

This museum of everyday life in East Germany recreates socialist-era interiors and displays examples of East German design, including a Trabant car that visitors can sit in.

2. Lustgarten

🚇 K5 🏛 Unter den Linden 1

Used as a parade ground for the German Democratic Republic, Lustgarten (Pleasure Garden) is now a popular park to take a break and relax after visiting the Museumsinsel. It is also a pleasant place for sunbathing.

3. WMF-Haus

🚇 L4 🏛 Leipziger Str., corner Mauerstr.

The former headquarters of the porcelain and cutlery manufacturer WMF has remarkable façades decorated with beautiful mosaics.

4. Alte Kommandantur

🚇 K5 🏛 Unter den Linden 1

Rebuilt with the original Classicist façade, this impressive building houses the Berlin offices of the media giant Bertelsmann.

5. Maxim-Gorki-Theater

🚇 K4 🏛 Am Festungsgraben 2
🌐 gorki.de

This renowned theatre was once Berlin's Singakademie, or singing school. Paganini and Liszt, among other great performers, are showcased here.

6. S-Bahnhof Friedrichstraße

🚇 K4 🏛 Friedrichstr.

Remodelled several times, this has always been one of Berlin's most famous stations. Between 1961 and 1989, it was the principal crossing point between East and West.

A display of transport at the DDR Museum

7. Komische Oper

🚇 K4 🏛 Behrenstr. 55–57
🌐 english.komische-oper-berlin.de

One of Germany's most magnificent opera houses, dating from 1892; it's closed for renovation until 2025.

8. Palais am Festungsgraben

🚇 K4 🏛 Am Festungsgraben 1
📞 (030) 208 40 00

The 1753 Baroque palace has retained its original elegant interior and magnificent ceiling frescoes.

9. Admiralspalast

🚇 J4 🏛 Friedrichstr. 101
🕐 Hours vary, chech website
🌐 admiralspalast.theater

Berlin's most legendary venue stages musicals and comedy shows.

10. Cold War Museum

🚇 K4 🏛 Unter den Linden 14
🕐 10am–8pm Mon–Sun
🌐 coldwarmuseu.de

Opened in 2022, this museum uses interactive displays to tell the story of the Cold War, which spanned more than 40 years, and the conflict between capitalism and communism.

Shops

1. KPM Store
📍 K4 🏠 Friedrichstr. 158
🕙 10am–6pm Mon-Sat 🌐 hpm-porzellan-shop.de/
The finest porcelain of the famous Royal Porcelain Manufacture (KPM) is on offer at this elegant store. Shop for vases, candle holders, cups and plates here.

2. The Square
📍 K4 🏠 Französiche Str.
🌐 thesquareberlin.de
This trendy concept store offers newcomer fashion and luxury labels such as Christian Louboutin and Stella McCartney.

3. Jack Wolfskin
📍 K4 🏠 Behrenstr. 23
🌐 jach-wolfskin.com
Make sure you stock up on clothing, equipment and footwear before setting out on any outdoor activities at this branch of Germany's famous outfitter.

4. Bucherer
📍 K4 🏠 Friedrichstr. 171
🌐 bucherer.com
A luxury outlet selling excellent quality watches and jewellery.

5. Karl Lagerfeld
📍 K4 🏠 Friedrichstr. 172
🌐 harl.com
Find refined, elegant accessories, shoes, bags and sunglasses at this luxury fashion label's store.

6. Nivea Haus
📍 K4 🏠 Unter den Linden 28
🕙 10am–7pm Mon-Sat 🌐 nivea.de
The Berlin flagship store of the German skin care brand Nivea offers a range of day spa services alongside selling Nivea products. Book facial treatments, massages and manicures, or simply buy some products to take home with you.

7. Kulturkaufhaus Dussmann
📍 K4 🏠 Friedrichstr. 90
🌐 hulturhaufhaus.de
A trove of books, movies and sheet music, Kulturkaufhaus Dussmann has a large section on classical music. The English-language section here is also excellent. It is open until midnight on weekdays.

8. Ritter Sport Bunte Schokowelt
📍 K4 🏠 Französische Str. 24
🌐 ritter-sport.com/de/berlin
The chocolate maker's flagship store has fun merchandise, a chocolate-themed exhibition and workshops.

9. Fassbender & Rausch
📍 L4 🏠 Charlottenstr. 60 🌐 rausch.de/en/chocolate-house
Giant chocolate sculptures of the Reichstag and Brandenburger Tor adorn the windows. There is also a café on the upper floor where you can try some of the store's delicious creations.

10. Mall of Berlin
📍 L3 🏠 Leipziger Platz 12
🌐 mallofberlin.de
The Mall of Berlin occupies an entire block and connects Leipziger Straße and Wilhelmstraße through a passage. There are 270 shops and restaurants.

The busy Mall of Berlin with shops and restaurants of every variety

Pubs and Bars

1. Newton Bar
🅿 L4 🏠 Charlottenstr. 57
📞 (030) 20 29 54 21 🕐 11am–2am daily (to 3am Thu–Sat)

One of the trendiest bars (*p78*) in town. Sink into the deep leather armchairs and sip your cocktails, surrounded by enlarged photographs of nudes by Helmut Newton.

2. Rooftop Hotel de Rome
🅿 K4 🏠 Behrenstr. 37 📞 (030) 460 60 90 🕐 Noon–11pm daily

The stylish bar on the roof of Hotel de Rome offers spectacular views of Bebelplatz and excellent Italian fare.

3. Zosch
🅿 J4 🏠 Tucholshystr. 30 🕐 4pm–3am Mon–Sat 🌐 zosch-berlin.de

An old-fashioned pub in Mitte, Zosch has an unpolished charm. Concerts hosted in the brick vaulted cellar range from folk to jazz music.

4. Einstein Unter den Linden
🅿 K4 🏠 Unter den Linden 42 🕐 8am–10pm Mon–Fri, 10am–10pm Sat, 10am–6pm Sun 🌐 einstein-udl.com

This Viennese coffeehouse-inspired bistro is popular with politicians, artists and journalists. Excellent wines and beer brands are on offer.

Einstein Unter den Linden, a Viennese-style bistro

5. Freundschaft
🅿 K4 🏠 Mittelstraße 1 🕐 6pm–2am Tue–Sat 🌐 istdeinbesterfreund.com

Enjoy a range of drinks at this cosy wine bar. This place specializes in mostly natural wines, mainly from Austria and France. Take a seat at the oval bar counter and order a glass, along with small dishes.

6. Café LebensArt
🅿 K4 🏠 Unter den Linden 69A 🕐 9am–11pm daily (to midnight Fri & Sat) 🌐 cafe-lebensart.de

More like a café than a bar, LebensArt offers tasty breakfast and afternoon cakes.

7. Ständige Vertretung
🅿 K3 🏠 Schiffbauerdamm 8 🕐 10am–1am daily 🌐 staev.de

The name harks back to the permanent West German representation in East Berlin. Ständige Vertretung is famous for its Rhineland specialities, such as Kölsch beer.

8. Bellboy Bar
🅿 L4 🏠 Mohrenstr. 30 🕐 6pm–3am Tue–Sun 🌐 bellboybar.com

Located on the ground floor of the Hilton Berlin, this plush bar has a wide range of food and drink.

9. Brauhaus Lemke
🅿 K7 🏠 Dirchsenstr. S-Bahn arch No 143 🕐 Noon–midnight daily 🌐 hm.lemke.berlin

Berlin's first craft brewery, this pub has a relaxed ambience and a variety of beers.

10. Windhorst
🅿 K3 🏠 Dorotheenstr. 65 🕐 6pm–1am Mon, 6pm–2am Tue–Fri,, 8pm–2am Sat 🌐 windhorst-bar.de

Sophisticated jazz bar with bartenders whipping up your cocktail of choice.

Restaurants

Enjoying the view from the waterfront at the Grill Royal

1. Grill Royal

📍K4 📍Friedrichstr. 105b 🕐5pm–midnight daily 🌐grillroyal.com · €€

Steak-lovers can choose from a range of cuts from around the world.

2. Crackers

📍K4 📍Friedrichstr. 158 🕐7pm–midnight daily 🌐crackersberlin.com · €€€

Head chef Stephan Hentschel serves up exceptional dishes at this stylish restaurant. An extravagant drinks menu makes Crackers a perfect spot for a late-night cocktail.

3. Bocca di Bacco

📍K4 📍Friedrichstr. 167–8 🕐Noon–3pm & 6:30–10pm Mon–Sat 🌐boccadibacco.de · €€€

A sophisticated Italian diner, Bocca di Bacco offers a wide range of fresh fish and meat dishes. This is also an excellent enoteca with a good wine list.

4. Liu Nudelhaus

📍L4 📍Kronenstr. 72 🕐11:30am–3pm daily & 5–7:30pm Wed–Fri 🌐chengduweidao.de · €€

The Sichuan noodles here are widely regarded as the best in the city. Expect to wait a while for a table.

5. Tausend Cantina

📍K3 📍Schiffbauerdamm 11 🕐7:30pm–late Tue–Sat 🌐tausendberlin.com · €€

Top-notch Asian and Ibero-American cuisine by celebrated chef Duc Ngo.

6. Restaurant & Café 1687

📍K4 📍Mittelstr. 30 🕐8am–1am daily 🌐1687.berlin · €€€

Enjoy modern European cuisine with Franco-Mediterranean influences. There's an extensive wine list on offer.

7. Borchardt

📍K4 📍Französische Str. 47 🕐11:30am–midnight daily 🌐borchardt-restaurant.de · €€€

A beautiful dining room makes for a stunning setting for the modern French dishes and schnitzel served here. Reservations are a must.

8. Cookies Cream

📍K4 📍Behrenstr. 55 🕐5–11pm Tue–Sat 🌐cookiescream.com · €€

This is the only vegetarian restaurant with a Michelin star in Germany.

9. Rotes Kamel

📍L3 📍Hannah-Arendt-Str. 4 🕐3–11pm daily 🌐roteshamel.de · €€

Fresh, satisfying meals and tasting plates, with flavours inspired by the Middle East, are on offer here.

10. Hugo & Notte

📍L4 📍Gendarmenmarkt 5 🕐Noon–10pm Tue–Sun 🌐hugo-und-notte.de · €€

Enjoy French cuisine at this restaurant on the premises of the French cathedral.

CENTRAL BERLIN: SCHEUNENVIERTEL

From the mid-19th-century onwards, the Scheunenviertel ("barn quarter") became a refuge for thousands of Jewish migrants fleeing Russia and Eastern Europe. After World War II the area was entirely neglected and that caused it to inevitably fall into decay. It has been rejuvenated in recent decades and many historic merchants' yards and narrow side streets have been restored, reviving the quarter's unique and lively character. With its many restaurants, galleries and shops, the district has become a beautiful and pleasant place to live and visit. The tragic history of its former inhabitants, however, remains unforgotten.

For places to stay in this area, see p174

1 Oranienburger Straße
🗺 J4 🏛 Mitte, between Friedrichstr. & Rosenthaler Str.

Located in the centre of old Scheunenviertel, Oranienburger Straße symbolizes the rise and fall of Jewish culture in Berlin like no other street. Traces of its Jewish past are visible at the Neue Synagoge (p101) and several Jewish cafés and restaurants. Some 18th- and 19th-century buildings attest to the street's former splendour – the Postfuhramt (p103) with its ornate façade, for example, or the house at Nos 71–72, built in 1789 by Christian Friedrich Becherer for the Grand Lodge of the German Freemasons. The area is also great for a night out – visit one of the many bars and restaurants (p106) lining the street.

The glittering carved dome of the Neue Synagoge

2 Neue Synagoge
🗺 J4 🏛 Oranienburger Str. 28–30 ⏰ 10am–8pm Sun–Fri (to 6pm Tue–Thu, to 5pm Fri) 🌐 cjudaicum.de 🚹

Once the largest in Europe, the New Synagogue (p59) was opened in 1866. In 1938, it survived Kristallnacht, when Jewish homes were vandalized across Germany, thanks to a brave guard, but it was damaged by bombs during World War II. Behind the splendid Moorish façades are a prayer room and the Centrum Judaicum.

3 Hackesche Höfe
🗺 J5 🏛 Rosenthaler Str. 40–41

Berlin's largest and most attractive group of restored commercial buildings, Hackesche Höfe extends from Oranienburger Straße to Rosenthaler Straße. The complex, comprising eight interconnecting courtyards, was designed around the turn of the 20th century by August Endell and Kurt Berndt, two leading exponents of the Jugendstil. The first courtyard especially has elements typical of the style: geometric motifs on vibrant glazed tiles cover the building. The complex has been carefully restored and is a popular centre of nightlife.

Various species displayed at the Museum für Naturkunde

4 Museum für Naturkunde

F2 **Invalidenstr. 43**
9:30am–6pm Tue–Fri (from 10am Sat & Sun) **naturkunde museum-berlin.de**

The Museum of Natural History *(p55)* is one of the biggest of its kind and features the largest dinosaur skeleton to have ever been discovered: a Giraffatitan found in Tanzania and housed in the museum's glass-roofed courtyard. Other smaller reconstructed dinosaur skeletons are also on display, as are taxidermist Alfred Keller's insect models, various types of fossils, meteorites and minerals.

5 Sophienstraße

J5 **Große Hamburger Str. 29**

Narrow Sophienstraße has been beautifully restored and looks just as it did in the late 18th century. The buildings and courtyards now have shops and arts and crafts workshops. Nearby, the Baroque Sophienkirche *(p104)*, the first Protestant parish church, was founded by Queen Sophie Luise in 1712. Next to it is a cemetery with some tombs dating back to the 18th century.

6 Brecht-Weigel-Gedenkstätte

F2 **Chaussestr. 125** **Hours vary, chech website** **adh.de/en/ archive**

Bertolt Brecht, one of the greatest playwrights of the 20th century, lived here with his wife, Helene Weigel, between 1953 and 1956. On display are original furnishings, documents and photographs.

7 Dorotheenstädtischer Friedhof

F2 **Chaussestr. 126** **Summer: 8am–8pm daily (winter: to sunset)**

This is a striking cemetery dating back to 1762. To the left of the entrance are the graves of Heinrich Mann (1871–1950) and Bertolt Brecht (1898–1956); further along are the pillar-like tombstones of Johann Gottlieb Fichte (1762–1814) and Georg Wilhelm Friedrich Hegel (1770–1831).

8 KW Institute for Contemporary Art

G2 **Auguststr. 69** **11am–7pm Wed–Mon (to 9pm Thu)** **kw-berlin.de**

Housed in a former margarine factory, this gallery displays works by established as well as up-and-coming artists.

JEWISH BERLIN

In the 19th century, Berlin had a population of 200,000 Jews, the largest such community in Germany. Apart from the wealthier Jews who lived in the west of the city, it included many Jewish migrants from Eastern Europe. They settled in Spandauer Vorstadt, primarily in Scheunenviertel, an impoverished part of the district. Later, Nazi propaganda used that name to denote the whole area to tarnish all Jews by association.

9 Gedenkstätte Große Hamburger Straße

📍 J5 🅰 Große Hamburger Str. 🌐 jg-berlin.org

Before 1939, this was a thoroughly Jewish street, with Jewish schools, the oldest Jewish cemetery in Berlin and an old people's home. The latter achieved tragic fame during the Nazi period – it was used as a detention centre for Berlin's Jews before transporting them to concentration camps. A monument commemorates the thousands who were sent to their death from here. To the left of the home is a Jewish school, on the site of an earlier school founded in 1778 by the Enlightenment philosopher Moses Mendelssohn (1729–86). To the right is the Alter Jüdischer Friedhof (old Jewish cemetery), where some 12,000 of Berlin's Jewish people were buried between 1672 and 1827. It was destroyed by the Nazis in 1943, and in 1945 it was converted into a park. Only a few Baroque tombstones or *masebas* survived. The spot thought to be Mendelssohn's tomb is marked by a *maseba*.

10 Postfuhramt

📍 J4 🅰 Oranienburger Str. 35

The richly ornamented Postfuhramt (post office transport department) dates from the 19th century. The building houses the head office of a medical technology firm.

Intricately designed façade of Postfuhramt

A DAY IN SCHEUNENVIERTEL

Morning

Take the S-Bahn to Berlin's former entertainment district at Friedrichstraße. Then walk north up to Reinhardstraße, opposite the Friedrichstadt-Palast, and turn left here towards Bertolt-Brecht-Platz. Continue south to Albrechtstraße to the **Berliner Ensemble** (p104). Admire the theatre where Bertolt Brecht used to work, then make a detour to visit his home, the **Brecht-Weigel-Gedenkstätte.** Return to Friedrichstraße and walk north to Chausseestraße. Then retrace your steps and turn left into **Oranienburger Straße** (p101) to fashionable Scheunenviertel. About a seven-minute walk down the street will bring the dome of the **Neue Synagoge** (p101) into view.

Afternoon

Walk down Tucholskystraße and turn right into Auguststraße for some refreshments at Strandbad Mitte (Kleine Hamburger Straße 16). After lunch return to Auguststraße. Picturesque courtyards are found here, such as the old-world **Schulhof** (p105) at No 21. Just across the street is the **KW Institute for Contemporary Art**. Continue along Auguststraße then turn right for the **Gedenkstätte Große Hamburger Straße** and the **Hackesche Höfe** (p101). Shop a little, then round off your tour of Scheunenviertel.

The Best of the Rest

1. Charité
📍 J3 🏠 Schumannstr. 20–21
🌐 charite.de
Many renowned physicians, such as Rudolf Virchow and Robert Koch, worked and taught at this world-famous hospital, founded in 1710. The Museum of Medical History (closed Mondays) has some 750 remarkable exhibits on display.

2. Alte and Neue Schönhauser Straße
📍 J5 🏠 Hackescher Markt
Alte Schönhauser Straße is one of the oldest streets in Spandauer Vorstadt. It is characterized by a colourful jumble of traditional and modern fashion shops.

3. Deutsches Theater
📍 J3 🏠 Schumannstr. 13A
🌐 deutschestheater.de
Once the place of work of Max Reinhardt, this theatre (p72) – considered one of the best German-language theatre – shows mainly German classics, often in new interpretations.

4. Berliner Ensemble
📍 J3 🏠 Bertolt-Brecht-Platz 1
🌐 berliner-ensemble.de
This theatre, established in 1891–2 by Heinrich Seeling, was the main venue for Bertolt Brecht's plays, including The Threepenny Opera.

5. Hochbunker
📍 J3 🏠 Reinhardtstr 20
🌐 sammlung-boros.de
One of the last surviving World War II bunkers in Berlin, Hochbunker is now home to the Boros Collection contemporary art gallery.

6. Monbijoupark
📍 J5 🏠 Oranienburger Str./Spree
This lovely park was once the grounds of the little Monbijou Palace.

7. Auguststraße
📍 G2 🏠 Between Oranienburger Str. & Rosenthaler Str.
The area around this road harks back to old Scheunenviertel, with courtyards and art galleries.

8. Koppenplatz
📍 G2 🏠 Near Auguststr.
In this small square, a monument of a table and an upturned chair recall the expulsion of the Jews.

9. Sophienkirche
📍 G3 🏠 Große Hamburger Str. 29
This 18th-century parish church preserves its old Berlin charm.

10. Tucholskystraße
📍 J4
This street is typical of the transformation of Scheunenviertel, with trendy shops next to renovated façades.

Strolling through the pleasant Monbijoupark

Old Courtyards

Ivy-covered exterior of the Sophie-Gips-Höfe courtyard

1. Sophie-Gips-Höfe
🚇 G3 📍 Sophienstr. 21–22
Famous for the Hoffman art collection, which is based here, this former sewing machine factory is a popular meeting place.

2. Sophienhöfe
🚇 G3 📍 Sophienstr. 17–18
The 19th-century red-brick artisans' workshops have been beautifully transformed into artists' studios and a theatre.

3. Heckmann-Höfe
🚇 G3 📍 Between Oranienburger Str. 32 & Auguststraße 9
These lavishly restored yards in a candy factory attract a lot of visitors. There's also a restaurant and trendy shops on the premises.

4. Sophienstr. 22 and 22A
🚇 G3
Two small inner courtyards, partially planted, are surrounded by yellow and red-brick walls.

5. Rosenthaler Straße 37
🚇 J5
This green-tiled courtyard is unique. Once part of the Wertheim department store, it now houses a boutique and tapas bar. The 1775 townhouse through which it is accessed has a beautiful wooden staircase.

6. Schulhof
🚇 G2 📍 Auguststr. 21
Time seems to have stood still around 1900 in this courtyard, which houses an elementary school.

7. Hof Auguststraße 5A
🚇 G3
The extensive courtyard of the former Postfuhramt permits a glimpse of the original façade of the building.

8. Rosenthaler Straße 39
🚇 J5
Berlin's post-Wall subculture of edgy art collectives is still alive and well in this unrenovated courtyard.

9. Kunsthof
🚇 J4 📍 Oranienburger Str. 27
A courtyard full of nooks and crannies, which is today occupied by a number of workshops, offices and cafés.

10. Kunst-Werke (KW)
🚇 G2 📍 Auguststr. 69
Large-scale installations by the resident artists are regularly on display at this well-known centre for contemporary art.

Rosenthaler Straße 39, a hot spot for Berlin street art

Pubs, Bars and Nightclubs

1. Buck and Breck
G2 Brunnenstr. 177 From 6pm daily buchandbreck.com
A bar with an intimate setting, this place specializes in fine cocktails.

2. Pawn Dot Com Bar
G2 Torstr. 164 6pm–2am daily (to 3am Fri & Sat) pawndotcombar.berlin
Whimsical cocktail bar in the yard of a former royal pawnshop.

3. B-flat
G3 Dirchsestr. 40 From 8pm Sun, Wed & Thu; from 6:30pm Fri & Sat b-flat-berlin.de
Live jazz, and occasionally dancing, are on offer at this small venue.

4. Reingold
F2 Novalistr. 11 (030) 28 38 7676 8pm–2am Wed & Thu, 8am–5am Fri & Sat
A relaxed bar with a 1920s ambience, Reingold is perfect for a nightcap.

5. Hackbarth's
G2 Auguststr. 49A (030) 282 77 04 10am–4am daily
This breakfast café transforms into a bar by sundown, serving beer on tap.

6. Mr. Susan
J5 Krausnichstr. 1 From 6pm Wed–Sat mrsusan.com
A cocktail bar serving creative drinks. It hosts occasional pop-up events as well.

Entrance to the Mein Haus am See, a chic retro bar/club

7. Anna Koschke
J5 Krausnichstr. 11 5pm–1am Mon–Thu, 5pm–3am Fri & Sat anna-koschke.de
This neighbourhood pub is popular with locals and students. The *bouletten* (meatballs) here are legendary.

8. Yosoy
J5 Rosenthaler Str. 37 From 11am daily yosoy.de
Tasty tapas, good wines and exciting cocktails are served at this attractively furnished Spanish restaurant – which is why it is usually crowded late into the night.

9. Mein Haus am See
G2 Brunnenstr. 197-198 mein-haus-am-see.club
Open 24 hours a day, this café and bar (p77) is popular with locals, especially on weekends. Reservations should be made online, in advance.

10. Oxymoron
J5 Rosenthaler Str. 40–41 From 10am daily oxymoron-berlin.de
This bar, club and restaurant in popular and lively Hackesche Höfe (p101) features chintz decoration and serves light German and international meals.

Enjoying a meal in the courtyard of the elegant Oxymoron

Restaurants

1. Chen Che

⓿ G2 ⓿ Rosenthaler Str. 13
⓿ Noon–midnight daily
⓿ chenche-berlin.de · €€

This Vietnamese teahouse-style restaurant offers fresh food and has a tranquil bamboo garden.

2. Rutz

⓿ F2 ⓿ Chausseestr. 8 ⓿ 6:30–10pm Mon–Fri ⓿ rutz-restaurant.de · €€€

Enjoy exceptional dishes created using local ingredients at this cosy restaurant (p78).

3. Monsieur Vuong

⓿ G2 ⓿ Alte Schönhauser Str. 46
⓿ Noon–midnight daily ⓿ monsieur vuong.de · €

This tiny Vietnamese snack joint serves great Asian dishes.

4. Frea

⓿ G2 ⓿ Torstr. 180, corner of Kleine Hamburger Str. ⓿ 5:30pm–midnight ⓿ frea.de · €€

This sustainable restaurant serves organic, plant-based food made using zero-waste practices.

5. Beth-Café

⓿ G2 ⓿ Tucholshystr. 40 ⓿ 11am–8pm Sun–Fri (to 5pm Fri) ⓿ adassjis roel.de/heute/beth-cafe · €

Small Jewish café of the Adass-Jisroel community, serving Jewish snacks and kosher wines and beers.

6. Hackescher Hof

⓿ J5 ⓿ Rosenthaler Str. 40–41
⓿ From 8am Mon–Fri, from 9am Sat & Sun ⓿ hackescher-hof.de · €€

One of the best restaurants in the area, Hackescher Hof serves tasty local food.

7. Bandol sur Mer

⓿ G2 ⓿ Torstr. 167 ⓿ 6–10pm Thu–Mon ⓿ bandolsurmer.de · €€€

A prestigious Michelin-starred restaurant, Bandol sur Mer

PRICE CATEGORIES

For a three-course meal for one with half a bottle of wine (or equivalent meal), taxes and charges included.

€ under €30 €€ €30–60 €€€ over €60

is casual with a bistro-style open kitchen. It offers flavourful French dishes that are beautifully plated.

8. Gärtnerei

⓿ G2 ⓿ Torstr. 179 ⓿ 6–11:30pm daily
⓿ gaertnerei-berlin.com · €€€

A chic Michelin-starred restaurant, Gärtnerei serves German dishes, accompanied by predominantly Austrian wines. The menu also offers plenty of vegetarian options.

9. Kamala

⓿ J4 ⓿ Oranienburger Str. 69
⓿ (030) 283 27 97 ⓿ Noon–11:30pm daily · €€

This hidden gem offers diners traditional Thai cuisine alongside an impressive wine list.

10. Coccodrillo

⓿ G2 ⓿ Veteranenstr. 9
⓿ 11:45am–2:45pm & 5:30pm–midnight Mon–Fri, 10:30am–1pm Sat & Sun ⓿ bigsquadra.com/en · €€

The all-Italian staff here serves traditional Italian food in a gleaming 1950s-style setting.

Tender pork knuckle presented elegantly at Rutz

CENTRAL BERLIN: AROUND ALEXANDERPLATZ

The area around Alexanderplatz – "Alex" to locals – is one of the city's oldest parts. It was here that the twin towns of Cölln and Berlin merged in the 13th century. The square defined the heartbeat of the city before World War II; after the ravages of war, it seemed vast and a little forlorn, but its vibrancy, described by Alfred Döblin in his novel *Berlin Alexanderplatz*, has slowly returned. A short walk away is the city's oldest coherent quarter – the 18th-century Nikolaiviertel – with its medieval Nikolaikirche.

For places to stay in this area, see p175

1 Rotes Rathaus

📍 K6 🏛 Rathausstr. 15

📞 (030) 90 26 20 32

🕐 9am–6pm Mon–Fri

Berlin's proud town hall (p61), the office of the Governing Mayor, is the political centre of power in Greater Berlin. It was built in 1861–9 to a design by Hermann Friedrich Waesemann on the site of an older town hall. The Rathaus was intended to demonstrate the power and the glory of Berlin, and the architect took his inspiration for the new building from Italian Renaissance *palazzi*. The building is known as the "Rotes Rathaus" (Red Town Hall) – not a reference to its Socialist past, but to the red bricks from Brandenburg province with which it was built.

Berlin's Alexanderplatz, overlooked by the Berliner Fernsehturm

2 Alexanderplatz

📍 J6 🏛 Mitte

The huge, largely desolate square in the centre of East Berlin, called "Alex" by Berliners, was one of the most vibrant places in Berlin before World War II. Alfred Döblin beautifully captured the rhythm of the city in his famous novel *Berlin Alexanderplatz* (1929). Not much remains today of the once frenzied atmosphere, although there is plenty of bustle around the Galeria department store (p113). Alexanderplatz was originally a cattle and wool market. Not many of the prewar buildings have survived – only Berolinahaus and Alexanderhaus remain, next to Alexanderplatz, the historic S-Bahn station, both dating back to 1929. The square was almost completely laid to waste in World War II, and most of the surrounding soulless tower blocks were built in the 1960s.

3 Berliner Fernsehturm

📍 J6 🏛 Panoramastr. 1a

🕐 Mar–Oct: 9am–midnight; Nov–Feb: 10am–midnight 🌐 tv-turm.de/en 🔗

This 368-m- (1,207-ft-) high TV tower is the tallest building in Berlin, affording views of up to 40 km (25 miles). There is a viewing platform at 203 m (666 ft). The Sphere restaurant above rotates around its own axis once every 30 minutes. The tower, visible from afar, was erected in 1965–9 by the East German government to signify the triumph of their capital East Berlin.

Colourful buildings and cobbled streets in Nikolaiviertel

4 Marienkirche

📍 J6 🏛 Karl-Liebknecht-Str. 8 🕐 10am–6pm Mon–Sat, noon–6pm Sun 🌐 marienkirche-berlin.de

Originally built in 1270, Marienkirche (p58) was extensively remodelled in the 15th century. Thanks to its Baroque church tower, it is one of Berlin's loveliest churches. Inside, the alabaster pulpit by Andreas Schlüter (1703) and the main altar (1762) are highlights. The 15th-century Gothic font and a 22-m- (72-ft-) long fresco from 1485, *Der Totentanz* (The Dance of Death), are its two oldest treasures.

5 Marx-Engels-Forum

📍 K5

This public park was founded by the East German authorities shortly after German reunification in 1989. The words "Next time it will all be different" were scrawled onto the bronze monument to Friedrich Engels and Karl Marx, the fathers of Socialism, erected in 1986.

Statues of Karl Marx and Friedrich Engels

6 Nikolaiviertel

📍 K6 🏛 Mitte Knoblauchhaus: Poststr. 23 🕐 10am–6pm Tue–Sun 🌐 en.stadtmuseum.de 🚻

Centred around the medieval Nikolaikirche (p161), the small and quaint Nikolaiviertel quarter with its nooks and crannies, souvenir shops and old Berlin restaurants is one of the most charming parts of the city. The area extending between the banks of the Spree River and Mühlendamm was razed to the ground in World War II. East Germany restored it after the war, but unfortunately not always successfully: some houses were covered in prefabricated façades. Knoblauchhaus was one of few to escape wartime destruction. Dating from 1835, it was the former home of the Knoblauch family (Neue Synagoge was designed by architect Eduard Knoblauch). Today it houses a museum depicting everyday life in Berlin, and includes a fully furnished apartment in the Biedermeier style.

7 Märkisches Museum

📍 L6 🏛 Am Köllnischen Park 5 🕐 For renovation until 2026 🌐 en.stadtmuseum.de

Berlin's municipal museum holds several artifacts relating to the city's culture and history, including architectural treasures such as doorways and the head of one of the horses from the top of the

Brandenburg Gate. There is also a Gothic Chapel room with a collection of medieval sculptures.

8 Ephraim-Palais
K6 **Poststr. 16** **10am–6pm Tue–Sun** **en.stadtmuseum.de**

This Rococo palace, built in 1766 for the merchant, court jeweller and mint master Nathan Veitel Heinrich Ephraim, was once regarded as the city's most beautiful spot. Rebuilt using original elements after the old palace was demolished, it houses a museum on local history and Berlin art history.

9 Karl-Marx-Allee and Frankfurter Allee
H3 **Mitte/Friedrichshain**

This avenue, lined with Soviet-style buildings, was built as a showpiece for Socialism in 1949–55. Known then as "Stalinallee", it provided ultra-modern apartments that are again in high demand today.

10 Neptunbrunnen
K6 **Am Rathaus**

The green Neo-Baroque fountain, dating from 1895, depicts the sea god Neptune. He is surrounded by four female figures, symbolizing Prussia's main rivers at the time: the Rhine, Weichsel, Oder and Elbe.

The magnificent, Neo-Baroque Neptunbrunnen

A DAY AROUND ALEXANDERPLATZ

Morning

Start your day at Strausberger Platz, where you can admire the Socialist architecture lining Frankfurter Allee and **Karl-Marx-Allee**. Then take the U-Bahn (or continue on foot) to **Alexanderplatz** (p109), where you can indulge in a bit of shopping before heading to the beautiful **Marienkirche**. Step back outside to admire the lovely **Neptunbrunnen** fountain, then walk to the **Berliner Fernsehturm** and – if the weather is nice – take the lift. Afterwards, stroll past **Rotes Rathaus** (p101) towards **Marx-Engels-Forum,** and head to **Zillestube** (p115) for lunch; the outdoor seating here is a particular draw.

Afternoon

After lunch, pop by the Schlüterhof, then cross **Schloßlatz** to walk along Friedrichsgracht and have a look at the old Jungfernbrücke. Then turn left into Neumannsgasse to find **Brüderstraße** (p112), which features two historic townhouses. Continue towards Scharrenstraße and Breite Straße and cross the Spree River at Mühlendammbrücke. To the left is the old **Nikolaiviertel** quarter. The Nikolaikirche museum is especially worth a visit. End your day with a meal at **Zur Gerichtslaube** (p115).

The Best of the Rest

1. Franziskaner-Klosterkirche
📍 K6 🏠 Klosterstr. 74 🕐 10am–6pm daily 🌐 hlosterruine.berlin

Remnants of a 13th-century Franciscan abbey, these ruins are surrounded by lawns, making this a picturesque spot for a break.

2. Stadtmauer
📍 K6 🏠 Waisenstr.

A fragment of the 13th–14th-century town wall that once surrounded the twin towns of Berlin and Cölln.

3. Palais Podewil
📍 K6 🏠 Klosterstr. 68
🌐 hulturprojehte.berlin/en/podewil

The light yellow Baroque palace, built in 1701–4, has been transformed into Podewil, a cultural centre and a subsidiary of the Grips-Theater (p70).

4. Stadtgericht
📍 K6 🏠 Littenstr. 13–15
🕐 9am–1pm Mon–Fri

The imposing municipal courts building features extravagant stairs in the lobby area, with curved balustrades and elegant columns.

5. Parochialkirche
📍 K6 🏠 Klosterstr. 67
🕐 9am–3:30pm Mon–Fri

Parochialkirche, by Johann Arnold Nering and Martin Grünberg, was one of Berlin's most charming Baroque churches, but the interior and bell tower were destroyed in World War II. In 2016, a replica of the tower was mounted, bearing a new carillon with 52 bells.

6. Märkisches Ufer
📍 L6

This picturesque riverside promenade gives a good impression of the city in the late 18th century. Look out for No 12, a typical Berlin Baroque house that was initially built on Fischerinsel in 1740 and transplanted here in 1969.

7. Heilig-Geist-Kapelle
📍 J5 🏠 Spandauer Str. 1

A beautiful example of Gothic brick architecture, this hospital church was built around 1300.

8. Ribbeckhaus
📍 K5 🏠 Breite Str. 36

The only Renaissance house in central Berlin, with a remarkable, lavishly ornamented façade.

9. Brüderstraße
📍 L5

This little street behind Petriplatz has a rich, historic past. Palais Happe at Brüderstraße 10 now houses the art gallery Kewenig.

10. Historischer Hafen
📍 L6 🏠 Märkisches Ufer
🌐 historischer-hafen-berlin.de

Moored at this port are several examples of the barges and tugboats that once operated on the Spree. The *Renate-Angelika* hosts a historical display on inland shipping.

Gorgeous atrium and grand staircase of Stadtgericht

Shops and Markets

The sleek Alexa shopping centre, home to top brands

1. Galeria

📍 J6 🏠 Alexanderplatz 9 🕐 9:30am–8pm Mon–Sat 🌐 galeria.de

The largest department store in eastern Berlin stocks everything your heart could desire. Its food department entices with a range of international gourmet foods.

2. Die Puppenstube

📍 K6 🏠 Propststr. 4 🕐 9am–6:30pm Mon–Sat, 11am–6pm Sun 🌐 puppen-eins.de

Adorable dolls made from porcelain and other materials await, as do mountains of cute fluffy teddy bears.

3. Teddy's

📍 K6 🏠 Propststr. 4 🕐 10am–6pm daily 🌐 teddy-laden.de

An old-fashioned toy store with probably the city's best selection of teddy bears, including brands like Steiff. It also has bear clothing and accessories.

4. Schmuck und Kunsthandwerk Berlin

📍 K6 🏠 Am Nußbaum 8 🕐 11am–7pm Mon–Sat 🌐 berlin-kunsthandwerk.de

A beautiful jewellery shop selling pretty rings, necklaces, bracelets and earrings, handcrafted using crystals from Swarovski and Polaris.

5. Manga-Mafia Store

📍 J6 🏠 Karl-Liebknecht-Str. 13 📞 (030) 61 65 34 57 🕐 10am–7pm Mon–Sat

A haven for manga and anime fans, this store offers a vast array of Japanese comics and art books as well as merchandise.

6. U- and S-Bahnhof Alexanderplatz

📍 J6 🏠 Alexanderplatz

This bustling area has a selection of shops for daily needs, plus late-opening fast food outlets and German *Imbisse* (food stands).

7. Alexa

📍 K6 🏠 Am Alexanderplatz, Grunerstr. 20 🕐 10am–9pm Mon–Sat 🌐 alexacentre.com

This centre houses some 180 retail outlets, such as Build-a-Bear Workshop, where kids assemble their own teddy, and LOXX, the world's largest digitally operated model train set.

8. Erzgebirgischer Weihnachtsmarkt

📍 K6 🏠 Propststr. 8 🕐 11am–6pm Mon–Sun 🌐 das-sachsenhaus.de

A vast array of stalls laden with a range of German handicrafts, including traditional wooden nutcrackers and Plauen lace.

9. Münzstraße

📍 J6

This tiny street is full of original fashion boutiques and designer stores. A real hotspot for fashion aficionados.

10. Wood Wood

📍 J6 🏠 Rochstr. 3/4 🕐 Noon–6pm Mon–Sat 🌐 woodwood.com/en

This store stocks men's and women's designer wear, plus its own line.

Wooden nutcracker

Pubs, Cafés and Beer Gardens

1. Zur letzten Instanz
K6 ⌂ Waisenstr. 14–16 ⏱ Noon–midnight Tue–Sun 🌐 zurletzteninstanz.com/en/start-en
Berlin's oldest pub dates back to 1621, and former guests include Napoleon, Beethoven and Angela Merkel.

2. Zum Nußbaum
K6 ⌂ Am Nußbaum 3 ☎ (030) 242 30 95 ⏱ Noon–midnight
This charming historic pub (p79) in Nikolaiviertel serves draught beers and Berliner Weiße in summer.

3. The Greens
H3 ⌂ Am Krögel 2 ⏱ 10am–6pm Mon–Fri, noon–6pm Sat & Sun 🌐 the-greens-berlin.de
A hidden café offering coffee, tea and snacks amid potted plants.

4. Brauhaus Georgbräu
K6 ⌂ Spreeufer 4 ⏱ 10am–midnight daily (winter: from noon daily) 🌐 georgbraeu.de
This beer garden offers rustic fare and beer from both Berlin and Munich.

5. Hafenbar-Fischerinsel
H4 ⌂ Märhisches Ufer 28 ⏱ May–Oct: noon–11pm Wed–Sun 🌐 hafenbar.business.site
This restaurant is on the deck of an old tugboat, the Renate-Angelika. Enjoy a beer here with potato salad.

6. Café Oliv
J6 ⌂ Münzstr. 8 ⏱ 8:30am–6pm Mon–Fri, 9:30am–7pm Sat, 10am–6pm Sun 🌐 oliv-cafe.de
Trendy Berliners get their organic sandwiches, flat whites and home-baked cakes from this sleek venue.

7. Café Ephraim's
K6 ⌂ Spreeufer 1 ⏱ Noon–11pm daily 🌐 ephraims.de/en
Hearty German food and excellent coffee and cakes added to the great views of the Spree River attract both locals and tourists.

8. tigertörtchen
K6 ⌂ Spandauer Str. 25 ⏱ 8am–6pm Thu–Tue 🌐 tigertoertchen.de
Come here for inventive cupcake creations such as date and walnut or crab and dill.

9. Marinehaus
L6 ⌂ Märkisches Ufer 48–50 ⏱ Noon–late daily 🌐 marinehaus.de
This traditional pub with maritime decor serves German food.

10. Hofbräu Wirtshaus
H3 ⌂ Karl-Liebknecht-Str. 30 ⏱ Noon–11pm Mon–Fri, 10pm–midnight Sat & Sun 🌐 hofbraeu-wirtshaus.de/berlin
Enjoy southern German dishes at this Bavarian beer garden.

Relaxing on a bench outside the historic Zur letzten Instanz

Restaurants

Colourful exterior of Mutter Hoppe, lit up at night

1. The Grand

📍 J6 🏠 Hirtenstr. 4 🕐 From 7pm daily 🌐 the-grand-berlin.com · €€

The lavish restaurant at The Grand is famous for its outstanding steaks.

2. Alois Moser – Alpenküche

📍 J5 🏠 Anna-Luise-Karsch-Str. 2 🕐 10am–10pm Mon–Sun 🌐 alois-moser.de · €

A cosy restaurant with an Austrian menu, Alois Moser has views of the Museum Island and the Berliner Dom.

3. Zur Gerichtslaube

📍 K6 🏠 Poststr. 28 🕐 11:30am–1am daily 🌐 gerichtslaube.de · €€

The former court building is a stylish setting for traditional Berlin specialities such as Prussian sausages.

4. MAMMAM Street Food Mitte

📍 L6 🏠 Inselstr. 8 🕐 11am–9pm daily 🌐 mammam-berlin.de · €€

Sample street-food-inspired dishes from Vietnam and Thailand at this cosy spot.

5. Zum Paddenwirt

📍 K6 🏠 Niholaihirchplatz 6 🕐 From noon daily 🌐 paddenwirt.de · €€

A must visit for fans of traditional Berlin food. The menu includes fried herrings and brawn, and a strong beer.

6. Zillestube

📍 K6 🏠 Spreeufer 3 🕐 From 11am daily 🌐 zillestube-niholaiviertel.de/en · €

Named after the 19th-century Berlin illustrator and photographer Heinrich Zille, this rustic pub serves hearty Berlin food and beers.

7. Fischer & Lustig

📍 K6 🏠 Poststr. 26 🕐 Noon–midnight 🌐 fischerundlustig.de · €€

With a large menu of fish dishes, Fischer & Lustig serves regional cuisine made with locally sourced ingredients. The courtyard tables are especially popular during summer.

8. Balthasar Spreeufer 2

📍 K6 🏠 Spreeufer 2 🕐 Noon–10pm daily 🌐 balthazar-restaurant.de · €€

Enjoy German and international cuisine with fusion dishes such as tagliatelle with a ginger and tomato sauce, and many more meat- and fish-based mains.

9. Fernsehturm Sphere

📍 J6 🏠 Panoramastr. 1a 🕐 10am–midnight daily 🌐 tv-turm.de/restaurant-sphere · €€

This revolving restaurant in the TV Tower offers superb views and Berlin-Brandenburg specialities, including cod with beetroot and potato purée.

10. Mutter Hoppe

📍 K6 🏠 Rathausstr. 21 🕐 From 11:30am daily 🌐 mutterhoppe.de · €€

Gigantic portions of delicious German food make up for the brisk service.

THE TIERGARTEN AND FEDERAL DISTRICT

In 1999, Berlin's green centre became the government district. Around the Tiergarten, Berlin's largest park, stand the Reichstag, the Bundeskanzleramt and Schloss Bellevue, the official residence of the President of the Federal Republic of Germany. The sprawling Tiergarten itself is a great place for strolling and cycling, and it also offers access to the Landwehrkanal, the Neuer See, the Spree River and Berlin's zoo. In summer, its lawns are used for picnics, sunbathing and casual sports.

1 Top 10 Sights
p117

1 Restaurants
p121

1 Hidden Treasures
p120

For places to stay in this area, see p175

The Reichstag, topped with a modern glass dome

1 Reichstag
More so than any of the other landmarks in Berlin, the Reichstag (p24), the seat of the German parliament, has come to symbolize German history.

2 Kulturforum
This unique complex (p46) of modern buildings features the best museums and concert halls in western Berlin.

3 Großer Tiergarten
🗺 L1 🚇 Tiergarten

The Großer Tiergarten (p66) is Berlin's largest park, straddling an area of more than 200 ha (494 acres) between the eastern and western parts of the city. Formerly the Elector's hunting grounds, it was redesigned in the 1830s as a park by Peter Joseph Lenné. At the end of the 19th century, the Siegesallee was estab-lished in the east of the park, more than 500 m (1,640 ft) in length, lined by statues of monarchs and politicians. After World War II, the starving and freezing population cut nearly all the trees for firewood and dug up the lawns to grow food. Thanks to reforestation since the 1950s, the Tiergarten, today, is one of Berlin's favourite green spaces.

4 Siegessäule
🗺 D4 🚇 Großer Stern 🚌

In the middle of the Tiergarten stands the 62-m- (203-ft-) high Victory Column (p61), erected to commemorate Prussia's victory against Denmark in the war of 1864. After victory over Austria in 1866 and France in 1871, the structure was crowned by a 35-ton gilded statue of the goddess Victoria. There are great views from the view-ing platform, 285 steps up.

5 Diplomatenviertel

⬛ E4 ⬛ Between Stauffenbergstr. and Lichtensteinallee as well as along Tiergartenstr.

In the late 19th century, an embassy district sprang up. Most structures were destroyed during World War II, and the buildings were left to decay until German reunification. After the government moved back to Berlin from Bonn in 1999, new life was breathed into the diplomats' quarter. Especially worth seeing are the Austrian and Indian embassies on Tiergartenstraße, the Nordic embassies on Rauchstraße and the Mexican embassy on Klingelhöferstraße.

6 Hamburger Bahnhof

⬛ F2 ⬛ Invalidenstr. 50–51 ⬛ 10am–6pm Tue–Fri (to 8pm Thu), 11am–6pm Sat & Sun ⬛ smb.museum ⬛

This former railway station (p57) is now the Museum für Gegenwart (Museum of the Present Day) and holds contemporary works of art. One of the highlights is the private collection of Erich Marx, with works by Beuys and others.

7 Sowjetisches Ehrenmal

⬛ K2 ⬛ Str. des 17. Juni

The Soviet Memorial was opened on 7 November 1945, the anniversary of the Russian October Revolution. It is flanked by two tanks, supposedly the first to reach Berlin. The memorial commemorates the 300,000 Red Army soldiers who died during World War II in the fight to liberate Berlin. A legend persists that the large column was made from the marble blocks of Hitler's Reich Chancellery. Designed by Nicolai Sergijevski, the column is crowned by a bronze statue created by Lev Kerbel. Behind the memorial, 2,500 Russian soldiers are buried.

8 Potsdamer Platz

Ravaged by World War II, Potsdamer Platz (p30) remained a wasteland for the next 40 years. In the 1990s, redevelopment began and this was one of Europe's largest construction sites, taking five years to build. Today, it is one of Berlin's busiest squares. Adjoining it is the Leipziger Platz, housing the Mall of Berlin. To the southwest is the Kulturforum, where you can find the Philharmonie (p46) and the Gemäldegalerie (p47).

PETER JOSEPH LENNÉ

Lenné (1789–1866), one of Germany's most influential landscape architects, was born into a family of gardeners in Bonn. He studied in Paris and joined the Royal Gardens in Potsdam as an apprentice in 1816. There he met Schinkel and together they set out to design the parks of Berlin and Potsdam in the harmonious style of the time.

Exhibition on Nazi Germany at Bendlerblock

9 Gedenkstätte Deutscher Widerstand

⬜ E4 🚇 Stauffenbergstr. 13–14
🕐 9am–6pm Mon–Fri (to 8pm Thu),
10am–6pm Sat & Sun 🌐 gdw-berlin.de/en

Today known as Bendlerblock, this 1930s complex lies behind the former Prussian Ministry of War. During World War II it served as the army headquarters. It was here that a group of officers planned the assassination of Adolf Hitler. The attempt failed on 20 July 1944 and Claus Schenk Count von Stauffenberg and others were arrested. Many of them were shot in the courtyard during the night. A memorial, created by Richard Scheibe in 1953, commemorates these events. On the upper floor is a small exhibition documenting the German resistance against the Nazi regime. The Bendlerblock has been incorporated into the Berlin branch of the Federal Ministry of Defence.

10 Villa von der Heydt

⬜ E4 🚇 Von-der-Heydt-Str. 18
🌐 preussischer-kulturbesitz.de/en

This late Neo-Classical villa, built in 1860–61 by architects Hermann Ende and G A Linke for one of the city's most elegant residential areas at the time, is one of the few extant examples of the architectural villa style typical of the Tiergarten. The Prussian Heritage Foundation now has its headquarters here.

The Sowjetisches Ehrenmal memorial to the Soviet Armed Forces

A DAY OUT AROUND TIERGARTEN

Morning

Start your tour of the Tiergarten near the **Reichstag** (p24). Explore the government district with the Bundeskanzleramt (Federal Chancellor's Office). Stop at **Käfer im Reichstag** (p121) for breakfast. You will pass the **Carillon** (p122) and the Haus der Kulturen der Welt on the way to **Großer Tiergarten** (p66). Continue along one of the paths into the park, until you reach Straße des 17. Juni. Turn right to go towards **Siegessäule** (p117). From there continue along Fasanerieallee until you reach **Café am Neuen See** (p67) for lunch.

Afternoon

After lunch, take a stroll through the Diplomatenviertel. From Neuer See, it is only a few steps east along Lichtensteinallee and Thomas-Dehler-Straße until you get to Rauchstraße with its Scandinavian embassies. On Tiergartenstraße you will pass the embassies of Japan, Italy, India and Austria. Head towards the **Kulturforum** (p46), then walk along Reichpietschufer until you reach the **Neue Nationalgalerie** (p46) to view works by artists such as Edvard Munch, Gerhard Richter and Andy Warhol. Stop for a meal at the Michelin-starred **Vox** (p121) at the Grand Hyatt.

Hidden Treasures

1. Neuer See
🔲 D4 🔲 S-Bahn station Tiergarten
Shimmering in a mysterious emerald green, the largest lake in the Tiergarten is perfect for rowing. Afterwards you can unwind in the Café am Neuen See.

2. Löwenbrücke
🔲 D4 🔲 Großer Weg
The Lion Bridge, which leads across a small stream near Neuer See, was built in 1838 and is "suspended" from the sculptures of four lions. This idyllic spot is a favourite meeting point in Berlin.

3. Lortzing-Denkmal
🔲 L1 🔲 Östlicher Großer Weg
There are 70 statues of philosophers, poets and statesmen in Tiergarten. The statue of the composer Lortzing, at one end of Neuer See, is one of the most beautiful.

4. Houseboats
🔲 K1 🔲 Str. des 17. Juni, Tiergartenufer
Docked on the banks of the Spree River are some of the few remaining houseboats in Berlin – an idyllic haven in the middle of the city's bustle.

5. Gaslights in Tiergarten
🔲 L1 🔲 At S-Bahn station Tiergarten
With 80 beautiful historic from different cities illuminating the paths, an evening stroll in the Tiergarten can be a romantic affair.

Scenic Schleusenkrug beer garden on the Landwehrkanal lock

6. Englischer Garten
🔲 D3 🔲 An der Klopstockstr.
The lovely English-style landscaped garden near Schloss Bellevue is ideal for strolling or relaxing at the Teehaus.

7. Locks
🔲 L1 🔲 At the Zoo, S-Bahn station Tiergarten
The two Landwehrkanal locks and the quirky Schleusenkrug beer garden are very popular with locals and visitors.

8. Estonian Embassy
🔲 E4 🔲 Hildebrandstr. 5
In a street next to the Greek Embassy, this building is characteristic of the diplomats' quarter.

9. Landwehrkanal
🔲 C3–G5 🔲 Corneliusstr.
Relax on the grassy banks of the 11-km (7-mile) long Landwehrkanal.

10. Carillon
🔲 K1 🔲 John-Foster-Dulles-Allee (Haus der Kulturen der Welt)
The *Carillon*, officially dedicated in 1987, is the largest of its kind in Europe The 68 bells are rung everyday at noon and 6pm in the 42-m- (138-ft-) high black tower. Open-air concerts are held on Sundays from May to September.

The Carillon, a sleek bell tower, looming over the trees in the Tiergarten

Restaurants

1. Café am Neuen See
📍 D4 🏠 Tiergarten, Neuer See, Lichtensteinallee 2 🕐 Mar–Oct: 9am–11pm daily; Nov–Feb: 10am–8pm Sat & Sun 🌐 cafeamneuensee.de · €

On the shore of the lake, this is a restaurant, café and beer garden.

2. Schleusenkrug
📍 D4 🏠 Tiergarten-Schleuse 🕐 Noon–midnight Mon–Sat (from 11am Sun, winter: to 7pm) 🌐 schleusenkrug.de · €

This café, next to a lock, has a beer garden and is popular with students.

3. Zollpackhof
📍 J1 🏠 Elisabeth-Abegg-Str.1 🕐 Noon–11pm daily 🌐 zollpackhof.de · €€

Huge beer garden with views of the Spree River, serving German-Austrian food and Bavarian beer.

4. Käfer im Reichstag
📍 K2 🏠 Platz der Republik 🕐 9am–4pm & 7–11pm Thu–Sat, 9am–4pm Sun 🌐 feinkost-haefer.de/berlin · €€

An ambitious restaurant, better known for its view than its food.

5. Joseph-Roth-Diele
📍 E5 🏠 Potsdamer Str. 75 🕐 10am–midnight Mon–Fri 🌐 joseph-roth-diele.de · €

Popular restaurant/bar serving traditional German food. Cash only.

6. Panama
📍 E5 🏠 Potsdamer Str. 91 🕐 6–11pm Wed–Fri, 4–11pm Sat & Sun 🌐 oh-panama.com · €€

The innovative dishes at Panama are perfect for tapas-style sharing.

7. Vox
📍 F4 🏠 Marlene-Dietrich-Platz 2 🕐 6:30–11pm daily 🌐 vox-restaurant.de · €€

An elegant restaurant in the Grand Hyatt Hotel, Vox serves a modern

fusion of Asian and international dishes. Do not miss the sushi.

8. Hugos
📍 D4 🏠 Budapester Str. 2 🕐 6:30–9:30pm Tue–Sat 🌐 berlin.intercontinental.com · €€€

Excellent gourmet food, stellar views and superb service combine to make this Michelin-starred spot one of the best. There's also a wine bar and private dining rooms available.

9. Paris-Moskau
📍 J1 🏠 Alt-Moabit 141 🕐 Noon–3pm & 6pm–midnight Mon–Fri, 6–10pm Sat 🌐 paris-moskau.de · €€

A classic restaurant serving seasonal dishes with an emphasis on game and seafood.

10. Facil
📍 L2 🏠 Potsdamer Str. 3 🕐 Noon–3pm & 7–11pm Mon–Fri 🌐 facil.de/de · €€€

This two-Michelin-starred gourmet restaurant focuses on Mediterranean cuisine. The rooftop dining area is surrounded by bamboo gardens.

Patrons enjoying traditional food in the beer garden at Zollpackhof

CHARLOTTENBURG AND SPANDAU

The sophisticated haute bourgeoisie enclave of Charlottenburg was the only Berlin district that did not touch the Wall. The historical streets off Ku'damm feature a range of stunning galleries, independent boutiques and tempting cafés and restaurants, many set within stout early 20th-century residential houses. The central section of this area and the proud town hall remind visitors that this was once Prussia's richest town, and was only incorporated into the city of Berlin in 1920. Spandau, on the other side of the Spree and Havel, is almost rural in comparison. Its late medieval core and hulking citadel make it seem like a small, independent town, far from the buzz of central Berlin.

1 Käthe-Kollwitz-Museum

This amazing museum (p43) provides a unique opportunity for visitors to become acquainted with the phenomenal works of the famous German graphic artist and sculptor Käthe Kollwitz (p64). Her drawings and sculptures portrayed the social problems of the poor, as well as human tragedy and suffering. The museum perfectly exhibits her work, including posters, sculptures and drawings, as well as letters and photographs

2 Zitadelle Spandau

🏠 Am Juliusturm ⏰ 10am–5pm daily 🌐 zitadelle-berlin.de 🔗
This citadel, built in 1560 by Francesco Chiaramella de Gandino, is sited at the strategic confluence of the Havel and Spree. The Juliusturm, a remnant of a fortress that stood here as early as the 12th century, was used as a prison in the 19th century. Later, the reparations paid by France after its defeat in the Franco-Prussian War of 1870–71 were kept here. The City History Museum of Spandau is located in the former arsenal of the citadel.

Admiring the Schloss Charlottenburg in the palace's gardens

3 Kurfürstendamm

This famous Berlin boulevard *(p38)* was known to be frequented by writers, directors and painters in the interwar years. Today it is a lively avenue lined with designer stores and elegant cafés.

4 Schloss Charlottenburg

The beautiful Baroque and English-style gardens of this lovely Hohenzollern summer residence *(p42)* are perfect for a stroll. After the damage caused by World War II, the palace's stunning interiors were restored.

For places to stay in this area, see p176

The red-brick Gotisches Haus in Spandau Old Town

5 Spandau Old Town

⌂ Breite Str., Spandau

When walking around Spandau's pedestrianized Old Town (Altstadt), it is easy to forget that you are still in Berlin. The narrow alleyways and nooks and crannies around the 13th-century Nikolaikirche are lined by late medieval houses, a reminder that Spandau was founded in 1197. The Gotisches Haus – the oldest house in Berlin, dating back to the late 15th century – stands at Breite Straße 32. It was built of stone at a time when most houses were made of wood. It is now the Visitor Information Centre, and some of its rooms are used to showcase finds from the house and other artifacts of the period.

6 Savignyplatz

⊙ C4 ⌂ An der Kantstr.

One of Berlin's most stunning squares is right in the heart of Charlottenburg. Savignyplatz, named after a 19th-century German legal scholar, is known as a district for artists and intellectuals as well as for dining out and entertainment. The square has two green spaces, either side of Kantstraße. It was built in the 1920s as part of an effort to create parks in the centre of town. Small paths, benches and pergolas make it a pleasant place for a rest. Dotted all around Savignyplatz are street cafés, restaurants and shops, especially in Grolman-, Knesebeck- and Carmerstraße. Many have lost their way here after a night out, which is why the area is jokingly known as the "Savignydreieck" (the Savigny Triangle). In the north, you can explore the attractive streets in Charlottenburg, including Knesebeck-, Schlüter- and Goethestraße. This is still a thriving Charlottenburg community; the shops, bookshops, and cafés are always busy, especially on Saturdays. South of the square, the red-tiled S-Bahn arches lure visitors with their shops, cafés and bars, particularly the Savignypassage near Bleibtreustraße and the small passageway between Grolman- and Uhlandstraße on the opposite side of the square.

7 Fasanenstraße

⚲ C5 🚇 Charlottenburg

Elegant Fasanenstrasse is the trendiest of the streets off Kurfürstendamm. Designer shops, galleries and restaurants are tucked away here, along with a retail strip catering to the masses. The junction of Fasanenstraße and Ku'damm is one of the liveliest spots in Berlin. One of the best-known places is the Hotel Bristol Berlin, formerly known as the Kempinski, at the northern end of Fasanenstraße. The former bank opposite cleverly combines a historic building with a modern structure. Next to it is the Jüdisches Gemeindehaus (p128), the Jewish community house, and a little further along, at the junction with Kantstraße, is the Kant-Dreieck (p63). The Berliner Börse (stock exchange), based in the ultra-modern Ludwig-Erhard-Haus (p63), is just above, at the corner of Hardenbergstraße. The southern end of the street has residential villas, some of which may seem a little pompous, as well as the Literaturhaus, Villa Grisebach, one of the oldest art auction houses in Berlin. There are also some very expensive fashion stores here, as well as a few cosy restaurants. At its southern end, the street leads to picturesque Fasanenplatz, where many artists lived before 1933.

Beautiful garden café in the Literaturhaus on Fasanenstraße

A DAY IN CHARLOTTENBURG

Morning

Begin your tour of Charlottenburg at Breitscheidplatz and head west along **Kurfürstendamm** (p38). At **Fasanenstraße** turn left to visit the Literaturhaus. You could stop for a mid-morning breakfast at **Café Wintergarten** (p130) in the Literaturhaus, before going back up Fasanenstraße in a northerly direction. You will pass the **Hotel Bristol Berlin** (p176) on the left, and on the right is the Jüdisches Gemeindehaus and the Ludwig-Erhard-Haus. Diagonally opposite across Kantstraße stands the **Theater des Westens** (p128). Turn left and head west along Kantstraße until you reach Savignyplatz. Explore the small streets around the square, such as Knesebeck-, Bleibtreu- and Mommsenstraße. Browse the shops for unique gifts. Northwest of the square is the Indian restaurant Ashoka (Grolmanstraße 51), which is a great place for lunch. Alternatively, head further west for lunch in Kanstraße.

Afternoon

Carry on west along Kantstraße to reach **Stilwerk KantGaragen** (p129), an interior design shop and art gallery. On your way back, visit **Der Kuchenladen** (Kantstraße 138) for cake and coffee. Head up Kantstraße and Jebensstraße to end your tour at the **Museum für Fotografie** (p126) and marvel at Helmut Newton's iconic Big Nudes.

The Funkturm, a popular landmark, with the ICC building in the foreground

8 Funkturm and Messegelände

📍 A4/5 🏛 Messedamm 22 🕐 10am–8pm Mon; tower: 10am–11pm Tue–Sun 🌐 messe-berlin.de ♿

The 150-m- (492-ft-) high Funkturm (TV tower), reminiscent of the Eiffel Tower in Paris, is one of the landmarks of Berlin that can be seen from afar. Built in 1924 to plans by Heinrich Straumer, it served as an aerial and as an air-traffic control tower. The viewing platform at 125 m (410 ft) provides magnificent views, while the restaurant, situated at 55 m (180 ft), overlooks the oldest part of the complex, the exhibition centre and the surrounding pavillions. In the east is the Hall of Honour, designed by Richard Ermisch in 1936 in the colossal Fascist architectural style. On the opposite side rises the silver ICC, the International Congress Centrum, built in 1975–9 by Ralf Schüler and Ursulina Schüler-Witte. Once considered one of the world's most advanced conference centres, it has fallen into disrepair and may be demolished. Nearby is the two-tier CityCube, Berlin's new trade fair and conference facility. The sprawling ExpoCenter grounds around it host International Grüne Woche (Green Week, an agricultural fair), Internationale Tourismus Börse (ITB, a tourism fair) and Internationale Funkausstellung (IFA, the consumer electronics fair).

THE HISTORY OF CHARLOTTENBURG

The magnificent Charlottenburger Rathaus (town hall) on Otto-Suhr-Allee is a reminder of the time when this district of 200,000 people was an independent town. The town, named after the eponymous palace, arose in 1705 from the medieval settlement of Lietzow. Towards the end of the 19th century, Charlottenburg – then the wealthiest town in Prussia – enjoyed a meteoric rise following the construction of the Westend colony of villas and of Kurfürstendamm. Thanks to its numerous theatres, the opera and the Technical University, the district developed into Berlin's west end during the 1920s.

9 Museum für Fotografie

📍 C4 🏛 Jebensstr. 2 🕐 10am–6pm Tue–Sun (to 8pm Thu) 🌐 smb.museum ♿

Helmut Newton (1931–2004), the world-famous photographer, has

A SPANDAU AND WESTEND WALK

Morning

Start with a journey on the U-Bahn. From the centre of town, take a U2 train in the direction of Ruhleben, and at Bismarckstraße station change to the U7 train in the direction of Rathaus Spandau. Ten minutes later you will have reached the centre of **Spandau Old Town** (p124), where you can visit Breite Straße and Nikolaikirche. Before returning to Charlottenburg, visit the **Zitadelle Spandau** (p122). Return by U-Bahn, getting off at the Wilmersdorfer Straße station, which is great for budget shopping. Stop for a fish lunch and a glass of Riesling at **Rogacki** (p129).

Afternoon

From Wilmersdorfer Straße a 30-minute walk west along Neue Kantstraße will take you to the **Funkturm and Messegelände** with the "Ehrenhalle". Take a coffee break on the city's rooftops at the **Funkturm-Restaurant** and enjoy the magnificent views from the observation deck. The Haus des Rundfunks (broadcasting house) nearby and the **Georg-Kolbe-Museum** (p128), a 25-minute walk away, are worth visiting. Then, take the S-Bahn to the **Olympiastadion** (p128). In the evening, return to Savignyplatz by S75 from S-Olympiastadion. End your day at one of the many acclaimed Asian restaurants on Kantstraße.

finally returned to his home city. This museum presents changing exhibitions of his early fashion and nude photography, as well as his photos of the famous, rich and beautiful, artfully captured from 1947 onwards.

10 Kaiser-Wilhelm-Gedächtnis-Kirche

🅳 D4

This Neo-Romanesque church is locally known as the Hollow Tooth, due to its wrecked condition caused by bombings during the war. A popular landmark church (p40) in west Berlin, it is also an anti-war memorial. The original western tower was the only building left standing on Breitscheidplatz after the 1943 air raids. Several efforts have been made over the years to preserve this grand ruin.

A mosaic at the Kaiser-Wilhelm-Gedächtnis-Kirche

The Best of the Rest

1. Georg-Kolbe-Museum
Sensburger Allee 25 ⏰ 10am–6pm daily 🌐 georg-holbe-museum.de

Sculptures by Kolbe (1877–1947) are exhibited in his home and workshop.

2. Le-Corbusier-Haus
Flatowallee 16

This innovative block was built for the 1957 Interbau trade fair. French architect Le Corbusier lived here.

3. Jüdisches Gemeindehaus
C4 Fasanenstr. 79–80 🌐 jg-berlin.org

The Jewish community house stands on the site of the Charlottenburg synagogue. It was damaged during Kristallnacht on 9 November 1938 and mostly destroyed during World War II. Only the portal remains.

4. Theater des Westens
C4 Kantstr. 12 🌐 stage-entertainment.de

Located in a building from 1895–6, this theatre (p72) is regarded as one of Germany's best and most picturesque musical theatres.

5. Technische Universität
C4 Str. des 17. Juni 🌐 tu.berlin/en

Berlin's Technical University was founded in 1879. It became a major intellectual centre and home to some of the greatest minds of the world.

6. Olympiastadion
Olympischer Platz ⏰ Hours vary, chech website 🌐 olympiastadion.berlin/de/start

Built for the 1936 Olympic Games, the stadium is an example of the Fascist architecture favoured by the Nazis.

7. Deutsche Oper
B4 Bismarchstr. 34–37 🌐 deutscheoperberlin.de

One of the most significant national cultural venues, this opera house (p72) specializes in Italian and German classics.

8. Denkmal Benno Ohnesorg
B4 Bismarchstr.

Alfred Hrdlicka's 1971 sculpture honours student Benno Ohnesorg, who was shot dead here during a protest in April 1967.

9. Universität der Künste
C4 Hardenbergstr. 32–33 🌐 udh.de

The School of Art is one of the best German universities for courses on fine arts, architecture and design.

10. Renaissance Theater
C4 Knesebechstr. 100 🌐 renaissance-theater.de

A gem of Art Deco architecture, this little venue has been run as an actors' theatre since the 1920s. A range of international and contemporary dramas are performed here.

The dancers' fountain in the gardens of the Georg-Kolbe-Museum

A wide range of sweet and savoury treats on offer at Lindner

Shops and Markets

1. Stilwerk KantGaragen
C4 · Kantstr. 127 · 10am–7pm Mon–Sat
A design and lifestyle store (p83) located in a converted parking garage.

2. Manufactum Store
C4 · Hardenbergstr. 4–5
10am–8pm Mon–Sat (to 6pm Sat) · manufactum.com
A unique store with a selection of classic textiles, furniture, garden tools, lamps and office supplies.

3. Peek & Cloppenburg
D5 · Tauentzienstr. 19
10am–8pm Mon–Sat
peek-cloppenburg.de
Offering five floors of men's, women's and children's clothing, this is one of Berlin's most popular stores.

4. Suarezstraße
B4 · suarezstrasse.com
To the west of Charlottenburg, this street is lined by around 30 antique shops. Visitors can find furniture, textiles, art objects and more.

5. TITUS Berlin Zoopreme
C5 · Meinekestr. 2 · 10am–8pm Mon–Sat · titus.de
The latest must-have labels are stocked at this streetwear store along with sports accessories and shoes.

6. Veronica Pohle
C5 · Kurfürstendamm 64 · 11am–6pm Mon–Sat · veronicapohle.com
This multi-label store specializes in evening and party dresses.

7. Bücherbogen
C4 · Stadtbahnbogen 593
11am–7pm Mon–Sat
buecherbogen.com
Berlin's leading seller of books on the arts and photography, Bücherbogen is situated under the S-Bahn viaduct at Savignyplatz.

8. Patrick Hellmann
C4 · Bleibtreustr. 36 · 10am–7pm Mon–Sat · patrickhellmann.com
Gentlemen's fashions made from the best materials, including Hellmann's own collection, and clothes from well-known designers can be found here.

9. Rogacki
B4 · Wilmersdorfer Str. 145/6
10am–6pm Tue–Thu, 9am–6pm Fri, 8am–2pm Sat · rogachi.de
Established in 1935, Rogacki is a famous seafood delicatessen.

10. Lindner
C4 · Knesebechstr. 92 · 8am–6pm Mon–Fri, 8am–1:30pm Sat
lindner-esskultur.de/lindner
This traditional store specializes in fresh delicatessen products.

A variety of coffees on display at Berliner Kaffeerösterei

Cafés and Coffee Shops

1. Berliner Kaffeerösterei

📍 C6 🏠 Uhlandstraße 173 🕐 9am–8pm Mon–Sat, 10am–7pm Sun 🔲 berliner-kaffeeroesterei.de

This place offers coffee beans from around the world, and cakes and snacks.

2. Café Wintergarten im Literaturhaus

📍 C5 🏠 Fasanenstr. 23 🕐 9am–midnight daily 🔲 cafe-im-literaturhaus.de

Based in the conservatory of an old city mansion, this beautiful café also has garden seating in the summer.

3. Manufactum Brot und Butter

📍 C5 🏠 Hardenbergstrasse 4–5 🕐 8am–7pm Mon–Fri, 8am–6pm Sat 🔲 manufactum.de

A bakery-café on the ground floor of the Manufactum department store.

4. Café Maitre Münch

📍 B5 🏠 Giesebrechtstr. 16 🕐 11am–6pm Tue–Sat (from 10am Sat) 🔲 cafe-maitre-muench.de

Expect homemade desserts such as cakes and macaroons, and a small but hearty mains menu at this cosy spot.

5. Café Hardenberg

📍 C5 🏠 Hardenbergstr. 10 🕐 9am–1am daily 🔲 cafe-hardenberg.com

A favourite of students and artists since the 1850s, this café has a great atmosphere and reasonable prices.

6. Balzac Coffee

📍 C4 🏠 Knesebechstraße 1–2 🕐 7am–8pm Mon–Fri, 8am–8pm Sat & 8am–7pm Sun

A German gourmet coffee chain serving speciality drinks and snacks.

7. Der Kuchenladen

📍 B4 🏠 Kantstr. 138 🕐 10am–6:30pm daily 🔲 derkuchenladen.de

Enjoy delectable lemon tarts and other delicious homemade delights at this tiny café.

8. Café Kleine Orangerie

📍 B3 🏠 Spandauer Damm 20 📞 (030) 322 20 21 🕐 10am–6pm Tue–Sun

A small, pleasant garden café at the historic building of Charlottenburg Palace serving light snacks and coffee.

9. Einstein Café Savignyplatz

📍 C4 🏠 Stadtbahnbogen 596 🕐 7am–8pm Mon–Fri, 8am–8pm Sat, 8am–9am Sun 🔲 einstein-kaffee.de

This branch of the Berlin café chain is located under the arches of the Savignyplatz S-Bahn station viaduct.

10. Schwarzes Café

📍 B4 🏠 Kantstr. 148 🕐 24 hours 🔲 schwarzescafe-berlin.de

This alternative rock café offers excellent all-day breakfasts and is often packed until dawn.

Restaurants

1. Francucci

🔲 C5 🏠 Kurfürstendamm 90
🕐 Noon–11pm Mon–Sat, 4–10pm
Sun 🌐 francucci.com · €€

This popular Tuscan restaurant serves
excellent pizza, home-made pasta and
creative meat and fish dishes.

2. Lamazère Brasserie

🔲 B4 🏠 Stuttgarter Platz 18 🕐 6–
11pm Tue–Sun 🌐 lamazere.de · €€

With an interior shaped like a tunnel,
this charming restaurant serves typical
French cuisine. Book ahead.

3. Eiffel

🔲 C5 🏠 Kurfürstendamm 105
🕐 9am–midnight daily 🌐 eiffel-
restaurant.de · €€

A spacious French restaurant with
outside tables and some traditional
Berlin and Mediterranean dishes.

4. Die Nußbaumerin

🔲 C4 🏠 Leibnizstr. 55 🕐 5–11:30pm
Mon–Fri 🌐 nussbaumerin.de · €€

Michelin-starred chef Johanna
Nußbaum's menu features Tafelspitz
(boiled beef broth) and Kaiserschmarrn
(scrambled pancake).

5. Kuchi

🔲 B4 🏠 Kantstr. 30 🕐 Noon–11pm
daily 🌐 kuchi.de · €€

This minimalist restaurant has a loyal
clientele and the best sushi bar.

6. Lon Men's Noodle House

🔲 B4 🏠 Kanstr. 33 🕐 Noon–10pm
Wed–Mon 🌐 lon-mens-noodle-
house.business.site · €€

The wait is worth it at this Taiwanese
restaurant, which has the best noodles.

7. Lubitsch

🔲 C4 🏠 Bleibtreustr. 47 🕐 10am–
midnight Mon–Sat, 6pm–midnight
Sun 🌐 restaurant-lubitsch.dem · €€

A small, elegant restaurant serving
fresh, regional cuisine.

PRICE CATEGORIES

For a three-course meal for one with
half a bottle of wine (or equivalent
meal), taxes and charges included.

€ under €30 €€ €30–60 €€€ over €60

---

8. Mine Restaurant

🔲 C5 🏠 Meinehestr. 10
🕐 6pm–midnight Tue–Sat
🌐 minerestaurant.de · €€

Enjoy contemporary Italian dishes
at this restaurant. The delicious
food is complemented by a terrific
wine list and amazing desserts.

9. Marjellchen

🔲 B5 🏠 Mommsenstr. 9 🕐 5pm–
midnight daily 🌐 restaurant-
marjellchen-berlin.de · €€

This delightful restaurant serves
hearty dishes from East Prussia,
Pomerania and Silesia.

10. Bruderherz

🔲 B4 🏠 Leonhardtstr. 6
🕐 Noon–midnight Tue–Sat
🌐 bruderherz-restaurant.de · €

A relaxed atmosphere welcomes
guests at this restaurant, which is
run by two Polish brothers. It
serves excellent pasta and other
Italian dishes.

**Outdoor seating at the
elegant Lubitsch**

KREUZBERG, SCHÖNEBERG AND NEUKÖLLN

Before the Wall fell, Kreuzberg was a hotbed of squatters, hippies and anarchists. Despite rapid gentrification it is still the city's most colourful area. Here, a diverse community of professionals, artists and students harmoniously coexists in renovated petit-bourgeois flats. The adjacent Neukölln is Berlin's trendiest area for art galleries, grunge-hip bars and clubs, particularly along Weserstrae. Schöneberg is not as daring as Kreuzberg, but it still evokes a free-minded spirit. Here, Winterfeldtplatz is lined with inviting pubs, and Nollendorfplatz is the nexus of Berlin's lively LGBTQ+ scene.

1 Top 10 Sights
p133

1 Restaurants
p139

1 The Best of the Rest
p136

1 Pubs, Bars and Nightclubs
p138

1 Shops and Markets
p137

Shipping and navigation exhibits at the Deutsches Technikmuseum

1 Deutsches Technikmuseum

📍 F5 🏛 Trebbiner Str. 9
🕐 9am–5:30pm Tue–Fri, 10am–6pm Sat & Sun 🌐 sdtb.de ♿

The history of technology and crafts is the theme of this museum (p54), located in the grounds of a former railway goods yard. Visitors can learn about developments in aviation and admire 40 planes, including a Junkers Ju 52 and a "raisin bomber", the type of plane used in the Berlin airlift. Old ships and steam locomotives hark back to the Industrial Revolution. A must-visit is the Science Center Spectrum, where you can perform any of the 150 experiments on offer. There is no admission fee for children after 3pm.

2 Jüdisches Museum Berlin

The Jewish Museum's unique architecture and exhibitions (p55) aim to illustrate the repercussions of the Holocaust. Narrow, slanting galleries with zig-zag turns evoke a sense of dislocation, and are punctured by "voids" – empty spaces embodying the vacuum left behind by the destruction of Jewish life. Nearly 1,000 years of German-Jewish cultural history are documented here; a special exhibition evokes everyday Jewish life in Berlin from the end of the 19th century. Visitors can hear the sound of a shofar, and listen to ancient and modern Jewish music at the Music Room. After undergoing extensive renovation, a permanent exhibition opened in 2020.

3 Haus am Checkpoint Charlie

📍 G4 🏛 Friedrichstr. 43–45 🕐 9am–10pm daily 🌐 mauermuseum.de ♿
Founded shortly after the Berlin Wall was built, this museum (p54) details the history of the Wall and the means people used to escape to West Berlin, from a hot-air balloon to a car with a false floor. Of the former border only a replica control hut remains.

4 Berlin Story Bunker

F5 **Schöneberger Str. 23A** **10am–7pm daily** **berlinstory.de**

Two exhibitions are installed in a former air raid bunker near the World War II ruins of Anhalter Bahnhof. The "Hitler: How Could It Happen?" exhibition tells the story of Hitler's rise to power, incorporating a model of the infamous Führerbunker.

5 Anhalter Bahnhof

F5 **Ashanischer Platz 6–7**

The giant structure was erected in 1880 by architect Franz Schwechten as a showcase station: official visitors to the Empire were meant to be impressed by the splendour and glory of the German capital. In 1943 it was damaged by bombs and in 1960 it was pulled down. The waste ground behind the façade was meant to become a park, but today the Tempodrom is based here, hosting concerts and cabaret shows.

6 Topographie des Terrors

F4 **Niederkirchnerstr. 8** **10am–6pm daily (May–Sep: to 8pm)** **topographie.de/en**

Between 1933 and 1945, three Nazi institutions of persecution and terror were located in this area: the Secret State Police Office; the SS leadership; and the Reich Security main office. After World War II, all the buildings were bulldozed. A striking documentation centre, designed by Berlin architect Ursula Wilms, was inaugurated in 2010 on this site, providing information about the headquarters of the National Socialist SS and police state during the Third Reich and showing the extent of the Nazi reign of terror throughout Europe.

7 Viktoriapark

F6 **Kreuzbergstr.**

This park *(p66)* was set up as a recreational space for workers in Kreuzberg in 1888–94 to plans by Hermann Mächtig. It has an artificial waterfall, and the Neo-Gothic Schinkel memorial, 66 m (216 ft) high, commemorates Prussian victory in the Wars of Liberation against Napoleon.

Remains of the Anhalter Bahnhof, once the gateway to south Germany

Allegorical figures adorn the mosaics on Martin-Gropius-Bau

8 Martin-Gropius-Bau

This beautifully ornamented former museum (p56) of arts and crafts often hosts contemporary and archaeological exhibitions.

9 Riehmers Hofgarten

🚇 F6 🏠 Yorchstr. 83–86

Over 20 buildings make up this estate, which was built as officers' quarters in the Gründerzeit, following the founding of the German Empire in 1871. Restored in the 1970s, it includes a pleasant hotel with an elegant restaurant.

10 Nollendorfplatz

🚇 E5

Nollendorfplatz and neighbouring Winterfeldtplatz are right in the centre of Schöneberg. The former square became a focal point for Berlin's LGBTQ+ scene. A plaque at the Nollendorfplatz U-Bahn station honours the 5,000 homosexual victims killed in concentration camps by the Nazis. Today, LGBTQ+ life is concentrated more in the surrounding streets than the square itself. Nollendorfplatz was a centre of entertainment before World War II. The Metropol-Theater, now a club, was then helmed by famed theatre director Erwin Piscator. The writer Christopher Isherwood, whose *Berlin Stories* became the basis of *Cabaret*, the musical and film, lived next door.

A DAY IN KREUZBERG

Morning

Start at **Anhalter Bahnhof**, which you can reach by S-Bahn. Then, continue along Stresemannstraße towards the **Martin-Gropius-Bau**. Wander around the exhibitions here, then take a break in the museum café. Afterwards, visit the neighbouring **Topographie des Terrors** exhibition, which will bring you face to face with the dark Nazi past of this area. Continue along Niederkirchnerstraße, passing an original section of the Berlin Wall. Cross Wilhelmstraße and stop at **Haus am Checkpoint Charlie** (p133) at the former East–West border at Friedrichstrasse.

Afternoon

Have lunch at **Sale e Tabacchi** (p139) in Rudi-Dutschke-Straße. Before you continue east, make a detour south on Lindenstraße to the **Jüdisches Museum Berlin** (p50) and the **Berlinische Galerie** (p57). Then take the U6 from Hallesches Tor to Platz der Luftbrücke. **Viktoriapark** nearby is a good place for a rest, or stroll up Bergmannstraße for a coffee break. At the end of the street, turn north into Baerwald-straße and continue to Carl-Herz-Ufer for a meal at the **Rutz Zollhaus** (p139) on the Landwehrkanal. Walk west along Planufer, turn left and cross the Kottbusser Brücke bridge to explore pubs between Kottbusser Tor and Oranienstrasse in the Kreuzberg district.

The Best of the Rest

Cycling on the Oberbaumbrücke across the Spree

1. Rathaus Schöneberg
🅿 D6 🄰 John-F-Kennedy-Platz

It was from this town hall in 1963 that US President John F Kennedy made his famous "I am a Berliner" speech, expressing his commitment to the freedom of West Berlin.

2. Asisi's Wall Panorama
🅿 G4 🄰 Friedrichstr. 205
🄾 10am–7pm daily
🅆 die-mauer.de/en 🄳

This is a life-size reproduction of the Berlin Wall as it appeared in the early 1980s, with sound and light installations.

3. Tempelhofer Feld
🅿 G6 🄰 Tempelhofer Damm 1
🅆 thf-berlin.de

Tempelhofer Feld (p84) became a public park when the airport here closed in 2008. The old terminal can be visited on a guided tour.

4. Mariannenplatz
🅿 H5

This park-like square with old trees is dominated by a large Gothic-style building. The former hospital and nursing school, Bethanien, is now a protected landmark and is used by cultural and social initiatives.

5. Oberbaumbrücke
🄰 Warschauer/Shalitzer Str.

Pedestrians and cyclists can cross to the other side of the Spree River from Kreuzberg to Friedrichshain on this red-brick bridge, one of Berlin's loveliest, which was built in 1894–6. The bridge provides views of the TV Tower and the Molecular Man.

6. Mosse-Haus
🅿 L5 🄰 Schützenstrasse 25

One of Berlin's most influential publishing houses was based in this Jugendstil corner house in the former newspaper district.

7. Friedhöfe Hallesches Tor
🅿 G5 🄰 Mehringdamm

Many celebrities are buried in these four cemeteries, including the composer Felix Mendelssohn Bartholdy and the writer E T A Hoffmann, whose work inspired Offenbach to compose his opéra fantastique *The Tales of Hoffmann*.

8. Gasometer Schöneberg
🅿 E6 🄰 Torgauer Str. 12–15

Once a massive gas holder, this Schöneberg landmark was decommissioned in the 1990s and turned into a viewing platform.

9. Kottbusser Tor
🅿 H5

This square in Kreuzberg is tucked away in between 1970s prefabricated buildings in the Turkish heart of the district.

10. Kammergericht
🅿 E6 🄰 Potsdamer Str. 186

From 1947 to 1990, this magnificent supreme court, built in 1909–13, was used as the Allied Control Council.

Shops and Markets

1. Winterfeldtmarkt
E5 ☑ Winterfeldtplatz ☑ 8am–4pm Wed & Sat (to 1pm Wed)

Berlin's largest market *(p83)*, located in Schöneberg, offers fresh fruit and vegetables, homeware, flowers and deli goods.

2. Türkenmarkt am Maybachufer
H5 ☑ Maybachufer ☑ 11am–6:30pm Tue & Fri

This vibrant, sometimes chaotic, market *(p83)* is the place to buy unleavened bread, fresh fruit and vegetables, and goat's cheese.

3. Wesen
T Tellstraße 7 ☑ 11am–7pm daily ☑ format-favourites.de

Find ethically and locally produced jewels, bags or shoes here, manufactured by Fairtrade fashion brands.

4. Oranienplatz and Oranienstraße
H5 ☑ Oranienstr./corner Oranienplatz

Kreuzberg's main square and unofficial high street specialize in all things alternative.

5. Winterfeldt Schokoladen
E6 ☑ Goltzstr. 23 ☑ 9am–8pm Mon–Fri, 9am–6pm Sat, midnight–7pm Sun ☑ winterfeldt-schokoladen.de

Choose from a variety of chocolates at this lovely store with an adjoining café.

6. Depot 2
H5 ☑ Oranienstr. 9 ☑ depot2.de

This small boutique sells the latest streetwear, trainers and hip-hop fashion by local labels.

7. Hard Wax
H5 ☑ Köpenicher Str. 70 Kraftwerk Berlin ☑ Noon–8pm Mon–Sat

This famous record store offers a carefully curated music collection.

You can find everything from dubstep and techno to reggae and disco.

8. Ararat
G6 ☑ Bergmannstr. 99A ☑ ararat-berlin.de

One of Berlin's best-stocked and trendiest stationery, curiosity and gift shops, the colourful Ararat has many designer items for sale.

9. Marheineke-Markthalle
G6 ☑ Marheinekeplatz ☑ 8am–8pm Mon–Fri, 8am–6pm Sat

This is one of the last remaining market halls in Berlin. Marheineke has colourful fruit and vegetable stores and a wide range of organic produce, as well as numerous snack bars.

10. Overkill
H4 ☑ Köpenicher Straße 195A ☑ 11am–8pm Mon–Sat ☑ overkillshop.com

With more than 500 pairs of trainers in stock, this wonderful shop serves as a paradise for all streetwear fans.

A large selection of trainers on display at Overkill

Pubs, Bars and Nightclubs

The well-stocked bar at Ankerklause in Kottbusser Damm

1. Ankerklause
⊙ H5 **⌂** Kottbusser Damm 104
ⓦ ankerklause.de
An informal and popular late-night bar and café on the Landwehrkanal.

2. E & M Leydicke
⊙ E6 **⌂** Mansteinstr. 4 **⊙** 7pm–1am daily **ⓦ** leydicke.com
This popular family-run bar (p78) hosts amazing parties.

3. Max und Moritz
⊙ H5 **⌂** Oranienstr. 162 **⊙** 5–11pm Wed–Mon **ⓦ** maxundmoritzberlin.de
A 120-year-old inn serving dishes such as Königsberger Klopse (braised meatballs with caper sauce) and rare local beers.

4. Van Loon
⊙ G5 **⌂** Carl-Herz-Ufer 5–7
⊙ 10am–11pm daily **ⓦ** vanloon.de
Savour a snack surrounded by nautical artifacts on this old barge moored in Urbanhafen.

5. SilverWings Club
⊙ F6 **⌂** Columbiadamm 10
⊙ 10pm–5am Sat **ⓦ** silverwings.de
Established in 1952, SilverWings (p76) is one of the oldest nightclubs in Berlin. It hosts various events and parties featuring rock 'n' roll and soul music.

6. Rauschgold
⊙ F6 **⌂** Mehringdamm 62
ⓦ rauschgold.berlin
Best visited late at night, this popular bar gets very crowded on weekends. It offers karaoke and themed nights with a mixed crowd.

7. Green Door
⊙ E5 **⌂** Winterfeldtstr. 50
⊙ 7pm–1:30am Mon–Thu, 7pm–2am Fri & Sat **ⓦ** greendoor.de
Do not miss out on the extensive drinks menu offered here (p78). Happy hours are from 6 to 8pm.

8. SO36
⊙ H5 **⌂** Oranienstr. 190 **ⓦ** so36.com
The SO36 (p75) is a very lively alternative music and dance club. Visitors can enjoy a range of concerts, shows and parties here.

9. Würgeengel
⊙ H5 **⌂** Dresdener Str. 122
ⓦ wuergeengel.de
The drinks at the "Angel of Death" are not lethal, but the bar staff and clientele are straight out of a Buñuel film.

10. Klunkerkranich
⌂ Karl-Marx-Str. 66
ⓦ klunkerkranich.org
This rooftop bar overlooks the city and offers stunning views at sunset. Take the lift to the top of Neukölln Arcaden, then walk the rest of the way through the car park.

Soaking up the view from the rooftop at Klunkerkranich

Restaurants

PRICE CATEGORIES

For a three-course meal for one with half a bottle of wine (or equivalent meal), taxes and charges included.

€ under €30 €€ €30–60 €€€ over €60

1. Defne

📍 H5 📍 Planufer. 92c 🕐 4pm–midnight daily (winter: from 5pm) 🌐 restaurant-defne.business.site · €

A restaurant with an intimate setting, Defne serves modern Turkish food. It does not accept credit cards.

2. Entrecôte

📍 G4 📍 Schützenstr. 5 🕐 11:30am–midnight Mon–Fri, 6pm–midnight Sat, 5:30pm–midnight Sun 🌐 entrecote.de · €€

Simple yet tasty meals are served at this French brasserie, located close to Checkpoint Charlie (p133).

3. Rutz Zollhaus

📍 G5 📍 Carl-Herz-Ufer 30 🕐 From 4pm Wed–Sat, from 1pm Sun 🌐 rutz-zollhaus.de · €€

Formerly a border control point on the banks of the Landwehrkanal, the Rutz Zollhaus serves international and German fare. Be sure to try the house speciality, *Brandenburger Landente aus dem Rohr* (roast duck).

4. Zola

📍 H5 📍 Paul-Linche-Ufer 39 🕐 Noon–10pm daily · €

Excellent Neapolitan-style pizza draws crowds to this quaint place with outdoor seating on the Landwehrkanal.

5. Lavanderia Vecchia

📍 H6 📍 Flughafenstr. 46 🕐 Noon–2:30pm & 7:30–11pm Tue–Fri, 7:30–11pm Sat 🌐 lavanderiavecchia.wordpress.com · €€

Set in an old laundry, this Italian restaurant excels in Roman tapas.

Restaurant Tim Raue's sophisticated interior

6. Restaurant Tim Raue

📍 G4 📍 Rudi-Dutschke-Str. 26 🕐 Noon–2pm & 7pm–midnight Tue–Sat 🌐 tim-raue.com · €€€

This two-Michelin-starred restaurant explores interesting combinations such as glazed partridge with Japanese chestnut. Reservations are a must.

7. Long March Canteen

📍 H5 📍 Wrangelstr. 20 🕐 6–11pm daily 🌐 longmarchcanteen.com · €€

A restaurant with communal tables and dim lighting, like a Chinese street kitchen.

8. Horváth

📍 H5 📍 Paul-Linche-Ufer 44a 🕐 6:30–10:30pm Wed–Sun 🌐 restaurant-horvath.de · €€€

Graced with two Michelin stars, this fine-dining restaurant serves elegantly presented Austrian dishes.

9. Frühstück 3000

📍 E5 📍 Bülowstr. 101 🕐 9am–4pm Mon–Sun 🌐 fruehstueck3000.com · €€

Excellent brunch spot serving savoury omelets and eggs Benedict with caviar. Book ahead.

10. Sale e Tabacchi

📍 G4 📍 Rudi-Dutschke-Str. 23 🕐 4–11:30pm daily 🌐 sale-e-tabacchi.de · €€

Elegant Italian restaurant where you can dine in the courtyard in summer.

PRENZLAUER BERG

Even when the city was divided, this former workers' district in East Berlin was favoured by artists and an alternative crowd. While it continues to exert a similar pull today, Prenzlauer Berg is being steadily transformed by young professionals and families. Cafés and restaurants have taken over tenement blocks around Kollwitzplatz and Husemannstraße, giving the streets an almost Parisian flair, while Kastanienallee, also known as "Casting Alley", is the place for stylish Berliners to see and be seen.

1 Top 10 Sights
p141

1 Restaurants
p145

1 The Best of the Rest
p144

Vast Neo-Gothic complex of Kulturbrauerei, designed by Franz Schwechten

1 Kulturbrauerei
🚇 H1 📍 Schönhauser Allee 36–39 (entrance: Knaackstr. 97) 🌐 kultur brauerei.de/en

This complex of buildings originally housed the Schultheiss brewery, one of the breweries that made Prenzlauer Berg famous. The complex, parts of which are over 150 years old, was completely restored in 1997–9 and has become a lively and popular spot. Cafés, restaurants, a cinema, shops and even a theatre have sprung up in the red and yellow brick buildings and the numerous interior courtyards.

2 Kollwitzplatz
🚇 H2 📍 Prenzlauer Berg

Once a quiet square, Kollwitzplatz is today the noisy heart of the district. All around the green square, locals congregate in the numerous cafés, pubs and restaurants. From the lavishly restored façades it is hard to tell that this was once one of the city's poorest areas. The artist Käthe Kollwitz (p64) once lived and worked at No 25 (now destroyed), from where she highlighted the poverty of the local workers in her sculptures, drawings and sketches.

3 Prater
🚇 H1 📍 Kastanienallee 7–9 🕐 6–11pm Mon–Sat, noon–midnight Sun

The Prater is one of the few remaining entertainment complexes that were once common in big German cities. It was built in 1837 just outside the original city gates, and was first jokingly called "Prater" after its world-famous counterpart in Vienna. A concert hall was added in 1857 and by the turn of the century it had become so popular that the nickname stuck. Today, you can enjoy beer and food at the restaurant (p144) of the same name.

4 Schönhauser Allee
🚇 H1 📍 Prenzlauer Berg

Schönhauser Allee, 3 km (2 miles) long and lined with shops and pubs, is the main artery of the district. Down the centre of the road runs the high-level viaduct of U-Bahn line U2. A couple of buildings are still in their pre-1989 state and give a good impression of the old Prenzlauer Berg, especially between Senefelderplatz and Danziger Straße.

Waiting on the platform at the Schönhauser Allee U-Bahn station

5 Wasserturm

🗺 H2 🏠 Knaackstr.

The unofficial symbol of the district is this giant 30-m- (98-ft-) high water tower, built in 1877 as a water reservoir, but shut down in 1914. The engine house in the tower was used as an unofficial prison by the SA. The water tower stands on Windmühlenberg (windmill hill). This round brick building has now been converted into trendy apartments.

6 Jewish Cemetery

🗺 H2 🏠 Schönhauser Allee 23–25 ⏰ 8am–4pm Mon–Thu, 7:30am–1pm Fri 🌐 jg-berlin.org

This small Jewish cemetery was set up in 1827, when the former Jewish cemetery in Große Hamburger Straße was closed. Two of the famous personalities who have found their final resting places here are the painter and printmaker Max Liebermann (1847–1935) and the composer Giacomo Meyerbeer (1791–1864).

7 Zionskirche

🗺 G2 🏠 Zionshirchplatz ⏰ 8–10pm Mon, 1–7pm Tue–Sat, noon–5pm Sun

Zionskirche, dating from 1866–73, and the square of the same name form a tranquil oasis in the middle of the lively district. The Protestant church has always been a political centre too. During the Third Reich, resistance groups against the Nazi regime congregated here and, during the East German period, the alternative "environment library" (an information and documentation centre) was established. The church and other opposition groups who were active at Zionskirche played a decisive role in the political transformation of East Germany in 1989–90, which eventually led to the reunification of Germany.

8 Gethsemanekirche

🗺 H1 🏠 Stargarder Str. 77 ⏰ May–Oct: 5–7pm Wed–Thu (or by prior arrangement) 🌐 ekpn.de

Outside this red-brick church, dating back to 1891–3, East German secret

interior of the Gethsemanekirche,
redesigned in 1961

police beat up peaceful protesters.
It was the starting point for the collapse of the East German regime.

9 Husemannstraße
🅙 H1 🅐 Between Wörther and
Danziger Str.

The East German regime undertook
a perfect restoration of this idyllic
street for Berlin's 750th anniversary
celebrations. A stroll through the
leafy roads lined with houses from
the Gründerzeit (the years after the
founding of the German Empire in
1871) is one of the loveliest ways to
experience Prenzlauer Berg. Ancient-
looking street lamps and signs, cobbled
streets, antiquated shop signs and a
few atmospheric pubs take visitors
back to the late 19th century.

10 Synagoge Rykestraße
🅙 H2 🅐 Ryhestr. 53
🌐 jg-berlin.org/en.html 🅓

Built in 1904, this spectacular
synagogue (p58) is one of the few
Jewish places of worship to have
survived Kristallnacht on 9 November
1938, the violent attacks on Jewish
property by the Nazis. The temple's
historic interior was built from
red bricks in the shape of a Neo-
Romanesque basilica. It is the best-
preserved and the largest synagogue in Berlin. There are guided
tours every Thursday.

The Jewish Cemetery with its
lush green cover

A DAY IN LES HALLES

Morning
Set off from the U-Bahn station in
Senefelderplatz (p144). From
here, explore the old tenement
blocks and backyards. Then
continue west along Fehrbelliner
Straße to Zionskirchplatz, and visit
the eponymous **Zionskirche**.
There are numerous cafés on the
square, such as **Kapelle**, where
you could stop for a coffee. Leave
the square via Zionskirchstraße,
then turn left onto colourful
Kastanienallee. At the end of the
street you could visit **Prater** (p144).
Then turn right into Oderberger
Straße, one of the area's best
preserved streets. Continue
along Sredzkistraße until you
reach **Husemannstraße**. Look
around the old Berlin streets,
you may find something
interesting to buy.

Afternoon
Stop for lunch at a restaurant in
Kollwitzplatz (p141): Gugelhof
(p145) or **Zander**, the former for
German and French cuisine, the
latter for imaginative fish speci-
alities. After lunch, walk along
Knaackstraße to the **Synagoge
Rykestraße**. From here it is a few
paces back to the **Wasserturm**.
Rest at the small green space
around the tower before contin-
uing along Belforter Straße and
Kollwitzstraße to Schönhauser
Allee. Finish your walk at the
tranquil **Jewish Cemetery**.

The Best of the Rest

Distinctive dome of the Zeiss-Großplanetarium

1. Greifenhagener Straße
H1
Not the most beautiful, but one of the best-preserved red-brick residential streets of old Berlin.

2. Pfefferberg
H2 · Schönhauser Allee 176
· schankhalle-pfefferberg.de
This alternative cultural centre is set in a former brewery and hosts concerts, performance art events and festivals.

3. Senefelderplatz
H2
The wedge-shaped square is named after Alois Senefelder, a pioneer of modern printing techniques. At its centre is a "Café Achteck", a historic octagonal public urinal.

4. Zeiss-Großplanetarium
Prenzlauer Allee 80 · Hours vary, chech website · planetarium. berlin
Gaze at stars, planets and galaxies under the dome of this planetarium.

5. Mauerpark
G1 · Am Falkplatz
The vast park near the former border, comprising Max Schmeling Hall and Jahn Sports Park, was built for the Berlin Olympic bid in 2000. Today, it hosts sports and music events, karaoke and a Sunday flea market.

A stall at the famous Sunday flea market in Mauerpark

6. Helmholtzplatz
H1
Along with the trendy cafés and bars, this area also has buildings reminiscent of a social housing programme.

7. Museum Pankow
H2 · Prenzlauer Allee 227–228
· 10am–6pm Tue–Sun
· museumsportal-berlin.de
This museum charts the history of the district and its poor working-class inhabitants in the 19th century.

8. Konnopke's Imbiss
H1 · At the southern exit of U-Bahn Schönhauser Allee
· 10am–8pm Mon–Fri, noon–8pm Sat · honnopke-imbiss.de
This legendary *Currywurstimbiss* was opened in 1930. The sausages served here are among the best in the city.

9. Oderberger Straße
G1–H1
This street is lined with cafés, boutique and historic buildings. The old swimming baths were renovated in 2015.

10. Thälmannpark
H1 · Prenzlauer Allee
One of few parks in the northeast of the city, dominated by Socialist prefabricated buildings. It has a monument to Ernst Thälmann, a Communist murdered by the Nazis.

Restaurants

. Oderquelle

G1 · Oderberger Str. 27 · 6pm–am daily · oderquelle.de · €

asic Berlin and German dishes are erved up in an alternative, relaxed etting in this quaint little *Kiez* neighbourhood) place.

. Kanaan

Schliemannstraße 15 · 6–10pm ue–Thu, noon–10pm Fri–Sun hanaan-berlin.de · €

Oz Ben David, an Israeli, and Jalil Dabit, a Palestinian, run this small egetarian diner offering Middle astern food. They claim to serve he best hummus in town.

. Lucky Leek

H2 · Kollwitzstra. 54 · 6–10pm Ved–Sun · lucky-leek.com · €€

xperience vegan dining here. There re no à la carte menus on Fridays and aturdays, but you can choose from he three- or five-course meals.

. Prater

H1 · Kastanienallee 7–9 · 6pm–midnight Mon–Sat, noon–midnight un · prater-biergarten.de · €€

urprises at the Prater include a beer arden (Apr–Sep), a rustic restaurant n the courtyard and free live concerts. redit cards are not accepted.

. Sasaya

H1 · Lychener Str. 50 · Noon–3pm 6–11:30pm Thu–Mon · sasaya-erlin.de · €€

Head to Sasaya for some of Berlin's est sushi. Reservations needed. Credit cards are not accepted.

Streetside dining at Gugelhof, a popular spot

6. Gugelhof

H2 · Knaachstr. 37 · 5–11pm Mon & Wed–Fri, noon–11pm Sat & Sun · gugelhofberlin.de · €€

Bill Clinton was once a guest at this restaurant. The menu features an original combination of German and French cuisine.

7. Osmans Töchter

H1 · Pappelallee 15 · 5:30pm–1am daily · osmanstoechter.de · €€€

This modern, family-run restaurant serves traditional Turkish cuisine.

8. Pasternak

H2 · Knaachstr. 22 · 9am–1am daily · restaurant-pasternak.de · €€

This Moscow-style venue has borscht, Russian music and vodka.

9. Schankhalle Pfefferberg

H2 · Schönhauser Allee 176 · 4–11pm Tue–Sat · schankhalle-pfefferberg.de · €€

Enjoy home-brewed beer and snacks such as *Treberbrot* (bread made with malt left over from brewing beer).

10. Anjoy

Ryhestraße 11 · Noon–11pm Mon–Sat, 10am–11pm Sun · maothai.de · €€

Enjoy traditional Vietnamese cuisine as well as an interesting tea menu at this pleasant restaurant.

BERLIN'S SOUTHEAST

Berlin's east and south are considered to be remarkably different in character. Friedrichshain, Lichtenberg and Hohenschönhausen in the east are densely built-up, with their old tenement blocks evoking stark memories of World War II and perhaps even more of life during the bleak days of the East German regime. Green Treptow and idyllic Köpenick in the far southeast, meanwhile, seem almost like independent villages and, together with the scenic Großer Müggelsee, have become one of the most popular day trip destinations for international visitors and Berliners alike.

For places to stay in this area, see p177

Charming Köpenick, beautifully situated on the banks of the Dahme

1 Köpenicker Altstadt and Köpenicker Schloss

◫ Schloss: Schlossinsel ◷ 11am–6pm Thu–Sun (winter: to 5pm) ◫ smb. museum ◪

As early as the 9th century, people had settled on Schlossinsel. The village

KAULSDORF

Kaulsdorf   MAHLSDORF

1/5

KAULSDORF SÜD   WALDESRUH

Mittelheide

⑤ Köpenick   Friedrichshagen
⑤

KÖPENICK   FRIEDRICHS-HAGEN
Spree   ⑧
②❶   ⑨
⑦   Kämmereiheide   Großer Müggelsee

stayed independent until 1920. Its coat of arms still features two fish, and the Altstadt (Old Town) on the Dahme River has 18th–19th-century fishers' huts. On 16 October 1906, Wilhelm Voigt, dressed as a captain, led soldiers into the Rathaus (town hall) on Alt-Köpenick, arrested the mayor and "confiscated" the municipal coffers. The "Hauptmann von Köpenick" (Captain of Köpenick) is commemorated by a statue (p151) in front of the Rathaus. The 1904 structure is a good example of Gothic brick architecture from Brandenburg. The charming Baroque Köpenick palace, on Schlossinsel in the south of the district, was built in 1677–81 for the future King Frederick I by Dutch architect Rutger van Langervelt. It now houses collections from the Kunstgewerbemuseum (p54).

2 Mercedes-Benz Arena

◫ Mühlenstr. 12–30/O2-Platz 1 ◫ mercedes-benz-berlin.de

The city's largest entertainment arena, seating 17,000 people, hosts pop concerts and shows of all kinds, as well as being home to the Alba Berlin basketball team and the Eisbären Berlin ice-hockey club.

3 Museum Berlin Karlshorst

◫ Zwieseler Str. 4 ◷ 10am–6pm Tue–Sun ◫ museum-karlshorst.de

World War II ended here on 8 May 1945, when Germany signed its unconditional surrender. Documents, uniforms and photographs, displayed in the former officers' casino, relate the history of the war.

Treptower Park, an attractive spot for Berliners on sunny days

4 Treptower Park
📍 Alt-Treptow

Established in the 19th century for the city's working classes, Treptower Park *(p67)* is known for its Sowjetisches Ehrenmal (Soviet Memorial). In April 1945, 7,000 Red Army soldiers who died during the liberation of Berlin were buried here. Beyond the mass graves is a 12-m- (39-ft-) bronze statue of a Russian soldier holding a child and a sword with which he has destroyed the Nazi *Hakenkreuz* (swastika) symbol.

5 Friedrichshain
📍 H2

This area grew rapidly during the industrialization period. It became an Allied target during the war and was one of Berlin's most damaged districts. After the fall of the Wall, Friedrichshain attracted a young population, and it is now one of the city's most popular areas, home to trendy design and media companies, bars, clubs, and cafés, mostly set around Boxhagener Platz and Simon-Dach-Straße. Its Volkspark *(p67)* houses Ludwig Hoffman's Märchenbrunnen fountain, and the wooded Großer and Kleiner Bunkerberg hillocks.

6 East Side Gallery
📍 H4 📍 Mühlenstraße 🕐 24 hours
🌐 eastsidegallery-berlin.de

A 1.3-km (0.8-mile) section of the Berlin Wall was left standing next to the Spree River. In 1990, 118 artists from around the world painted onto the concrete, making it a unique work of art *(p85)*. Particularly famous is a mural by Russian Dmitri Vrubel showing Erich Honecker and Leonid Brezhnev kissing. Most murals were restored by the original artists in 2009.

7 Tierpark Berlin
📍 Am Tierpark 125 🕐 Hours vary, check website 🌐 tierpark-berlin.de/tierparh 🗓

Located in the Friedrichsfelde Palace park, Europe's largest zoological garden *(p67)* hosts several rare species. The Siberian tigers in their rocky outdoor enclosures are worth a visit. The park is known for its successful elephant breeding programme. The 1695 palace sits in the middle of this estate.

8 Gedenkstätte Hohenschönhausen
📍 Genslerstr. 66 🌐 en.stiftung-hsh.de 🗓

This former secret police prison for political prisoners was in use until 1990. Before 1951, it served as a reception centre for the Red Army. You can visit the watchtowers and cells – particularly horrifying are the windowless "submarine cells" for solitary confinement and torture. Guided tours in English are available from 11:45am, 2:15pm & 3:45pm daily.

9 Großer Müggelsee

🚇 Treptow-Köpenich district

Nicknamed Berlin's "Large Bathtub", the Großer Müggelsee is the city's biggest lake. Müggelsee is not as popular as Großer Wannsee, mainly because it is further from the centre. It is known for the beer gardens on its south side, which can be reached on foot or by boat from Friedrichshagen. You can swim in the lake, and around it are great walking and cycling paths.

10 Stasi-Museum Berlin

🚇 Ruschestr. 103, Haus 1
🕙 10am–6pm Mon–Fri, 11am–6pm Sat & Sun 🌐 stasimuseum.de 🚻

The former headquarters of the Stasi, East Germany's secret police, is now a memorial to the victims of the East German regime and of Erich Mielke, the minister in charge of the secret police. Visitors can see his offices, the canteen and spying equipment used by the Socialist regime.

A button spy camera exhibited at the Stasi-Museum Berlin

A DAY IN BERLIN'S SOUTHEAST

Morning

Begin your tour at Alexanderplatz. Sights on this tour are not always near each other, so using public transport is recommended.
Take the U-Bahn line U5 to Magdalenenstraße station, from where it is a short walk to the **Stasi-Museum Berlin**. Return to the station and continue on U5 to **Tierpark Berlin**, and explore both the zoological garden and the Schloss Friedrichsfelde, built in early Neo-Classical style. Then catch bus No. 296 from the Tierpark U-Bahn station to the Deutsch-Russisches Museum.

Afternoon

From the museum, either walk (15 minutes) or take bus No. 296 southwest down Rheinsteinstraße to the S Karlshorst tram stop. No. 27 goes direct to Rathaus Köpenick. Stop for a German meal in the **Ratskeller** (p151), the town hall's cellar restaurant. Afterwards explore **Köpenick Old Town** (p147). The old fishing village is especially worth a visit. There are many cafés near **Köpenicker Schloss** (p147). Continue your journey by tram No. 60 to Friedrichshagen, the access point for the Großer Müggelsee. From here take one of the tourist boats for a trip around the lake before returning to Köpenick for the train back to the centre.

The Matrix club, in the basement of the Warschauer Straße railway station

Bars and Nightclubs

1. Berghain
📍 Am Wriezener Bahnhof
🕐 10pm–6am Thu & Fri,
24 hrs Sat 🌐 berghain.berlin
This club has a good sound system and a cool crowd. The door policy is strict.

2. Arena
📍 Eichenstr. 4 🌐 arena.berlin
A riverside complex, Arena includes concert halls, a club ship (*Hoppetosse*) and a moored swimming pool (*Badeschiff*).

3. Cassiopeia
📍 Revaler Str. 99 🕐 From 10pm
Thu–Sat 🌐 cassiopeia-berlin.de
This underground urban enclave is for ungentrified clubbing and live gigs.

4. Sisyphos
📍 Hauptstraße 15 🌐 sisyphos-berlin.net
Inside a former factory, this large techno club is famous for its parties.

5. Matrix
📍 Warschauer Platz 18 🕐 10pm–5am daily 🌐 matrix-berlin.de
A popular club, Matrix attracts a young crowd and Berlin's best DJs.

6. Festsaal Kreuzberg
📍 Am Flutgraben 2 🕐 5–11pm
Thu & Sun, 5pm–1am Fri & Sat
🌐 festsaal-kreuzberg.de
This venue hosts rock, alternative and indie bands. It has a lovely beer garden.

7. Monster Ronson's Ichiban Karaoke Bar
📍 Warschauer Str. 34 🕐 From 7pm
daily 🌐 karaokemonster.de
At this lively bar, karaoke fans either practise their art in soundproof booths that can fit up to 16 people, or sing on a stage. Try the brunch on Sundays.

8. Salon zur Wilden Renate
📍 Alt Stralau 70 🕐 From 6pm Wed–Sun 🌐 renate.cc
Styled like a living room, this club plays house and techno music. It gets crowded shortly after opening.

9. Zenner
📍 Alt Treptow 15 🕐 Noon–9pm
Mon–Thu, 11am–10pm Fri–Sun
🌐 zenner.berlin
One of the largest and oldest beer gardens in Berlin, Zenner is a leafy space situated in Treptower Park on the Spree River. There is also a hall where live music events take place on weekends.

10. Revier Südost
📍 Schnellerstr. 137 🕐 4–11pm
Mon–Thu, 4pm–1am Fri–Sun)
🌐 reviersuedost.de
Set in the premises of the former Bärenquell brewery in the up-and-coming neighbourhood Schöneweide, Revier Südost hosts club nights, concerts and theatre and art events.

Restaurants

1. Il Ritrovo
Gabriel-Max-Str. 2 ◷ Noon–midnight daily ⊞ ritrovo.de · €

Enjoy delicious, well-priced wood-fired pizza in a friendly and cosy atmosphere. There is also a wine bar here.

2. Ratskeller Köpenick
Alt-Köpenick 21 ◷ 11am–11pm Tue–Sat, 11am–10pm Sun ⊞ ratsheller-hoepenich.de · €€

Traditional fare is served in the vaulted cellars where Wilhelm Voigt famously conned (p147) local civil servants.

3. Klipper Schiffsrestaurant
Bulgarische Str. 90 ◷ 10am–1am daily ⊞ hlipper-berlin.de · €

This two-masted 1890 boat has been turned into a restaurant; the menu features fish and game dishes.

4. Freischwimmer
Vor dem Schlesischen Tor 2 ◷ From noon Mon–Fri, from 10am Sat & Sun ⊞ freischwimmer-berlin.com · €€

Head for brunch at this restaurant and bar floating on a wooden terrace.

5. Burgeramt
Krossener Str. 21–22 ◷ Noon–midnight daily ⊞ burgeramt.com · €

A wide variety of burgers are available at this burger joint, from beef patties to many vegetarian options.

6. Khao Taan
Gryphiusstr. 10 ◷ 6–10pm Tue–Sat ⊞ hhaotaan.com · €€

Impeccable Thai dishes served as a set menu. Diners need to book weeks in advance to secure a table here.

7. Krokodil
Gartenstr. 46–48 ◷ 4–11pm Mon–Fri, 3–11pm Sat, noon–11pm Sun ⊞ der-coepenicher.de · €

Situated in Köpenick's Old Town, near the river baths in Gartenstraße, this is one of the nicest garden venues, especially in summer.

8. Bräustübl
Müggelseedamm 164 ◷ Noon–10pm Mon–Sat, from 11am Sun ⊞ braeustuebl.wixsite.com · €

This popular beer garden, belonging to the neighbouring Berliner Bürger-Brau brewery, serves excellent game dishes.

9. Hafenküche
Zur alten Flußbadeanstalt 5 ◷ 6–11pm Wed–Fri, noon–11pm Sat & Sun ⊞ hafenhueche.de · €€

Tucked away in the waterfront east of the Spree River, this port restaurant serves casual meals. The picnic baskets on offer are perfect to take on a weekend ride in a boat hired from the neighbouring shop.

10. Jäger & Lustig
Grünberger Str. 1 ◷ Noon–midnight daily ⊞ jaeger undlustig.de · €€

A rustic restaurant and beer garden, Jäger & Lustig specializes in typical German cuisine; options include game and some vegetarian dishes.

Freischwimmer, a waterside restaurant on the Flutgraben Canal

GRUNEWALD AND DAHLEM

Berlin's green southwest, which includes the districts of Grunewald and Dahlem, is dotted with scenic lakes, rivers, residential villas, private estates and small castles. Grunewald and Dahlem have a charming suburban character that has always drawn affluent and famous Berliners. Visitors can enjoy extensive walks in the Grunewald forest, take a ferry ride across picturesque Wannsee to the romantic ruins at Pfaueninsel or relax at Europe's largest inland beach. Dahlem's Museum of Europäischer Kulturen has a terrific collection, while the Haus der Wannsee Konferenz and Alliiertenmuseum recall a darker period in Berlin's history.

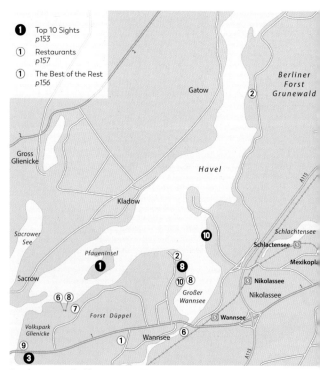

1 Top 10 Sights
p153

1 Restaurants
p157

1 The Best of the Rest
p156

For places to stay in this area, see p177

Friedrich Wilhelm II's palace on Pfaueninsel

1 Pfaueninsel

📍 Pfaueninselchaussee
🌐 spsg.de

Visitors to Pfaueninsel (p66) are immediately enchanted by Friedrich Wilhem II's romantic palace and the eponymous peacocks that run around here. The Wannsee island, which can only be reached by ferry, is one of the most charming spots for a walk in Berlin.

2 Museum Europäischer Kulturen

📍 Arnimallee 25 🕐 10am–5pm Tue–Fri, 11am–6pm Sat & Sun
🌐 smb.museum 🚻

Out of the three museums that once had a home in Dahlem, only the Museum of European Cultures remains today (the Museum of Asian Art and the Museum of Ethnology moved to the Humboldt Forum (p91) in 2021). The museum's vast array of objects on display, including graphic art and jewellery, represent life in Germany and other European countries from the 18th century to the present day.

3 Schloss Glienicke

📍 Königstr. 36 🕐 Apr–Oct: 10am–6pm Tue–Sun, Nov, Dec & Mar: 10am–5pm Sat & Sun 🌐 spsg.de 🚻

One of Berlin's most beautiful Hohenzollern palaces, the Schloss Glienicke is a romantic castle built by Schinkel in 1824–60. It served as a summer residence for Prince Carl of Prussia. The landscaped garden was designed by Lenné and includes pavilions called "Große" and "Kleine Neugierde" (large and small curiosity), a restaurant and the Orangerie.

Schloss Glienicke, detail

A reconstructed medieval village at Museumsdorf Düppel

4 Museumsdorf Düppel
🏠 Clauertstr. 11 🕐 Late Mar–Oct: 10am–6pm Sat & Sun 🌐 dueppel.de 🔗

This lively open-air museum serves as a reminder that Berlin was once a series of villages dating back to the 13th century. Costumed actors enact the daily life of the Middle Ages, with bread-baking, pottery and basket-weaving demonstrations. The gardens are fascinating.

5 Alliiertenmuseum
🏠 Clayallee 135 🕐 10am–6pm Sun–Tue 🌐 alliiertenmuseum.de/en

This museum recalls the 50 or so years of partnership between West Berliners and the Western Allies. Based in a former US barracks, it uses uniforms, documents, weapons and military equipment to tell the story of Berlin's post-war history, though not only from the military point of view.

6 Grunewald Villas
Some of Berlin's most attractive 19th-century villas are found in the streets around the Grunewald S-Bahn station. Especially worth seeing are Nos 15 and 11 in Winklerstraße, the latter of which was built by Hermann Muthesius in the style of an English country house. Villa Maren at No 12 is a beautiful example of the Neo-Renaissance style. The villas on Furtwänglerstraße and Toni-Lessler-Straße are also worth visiting.

7 Jagdschloss Grunewald
🏠 Hüttenweg 100, Grunewaldsee 🕐 Apr–Oct: 10am–6pm Tue–Sun; Nov, Dec & Mar: tours only, 10am–4pm Sat & Sun 🌐 spsg.de 🔗🔗

This small white 1542 palace is the oldest of its kind in the city area. It was once a hunting lodge for the Electors. Built in the Renaissance and Baroque styles, it holds paintings by Cranach the Elder and 16th–19th-century portraits of Hohenzollern rulers.

8 Haus der Wannsee-Konferenz
🏠 Am Großen Wannsee 56–58 🕐 10am–6pm daily 🌐 ghwk.de

It is hard to believe that something as abhorrent as the Holocaust could have been planned at this elegant villa. Built by Paul Baumgarten in 1914–15 in Neo-Baroque style for businessman Ernst Marlier, it hosted the Nazi elite, among them the infamous Adolf Eichmann, on 20 January 1942. They met to discuss the details of the mass extermination of the Jews.

Sunseekers relaxing on the sands at Strandbad Wannsee

An exhibition documents the conference and its consequences, as well as the history of the villa.

9 Mexikoplatz

Idyllic Mexikoplatz in the southern district of Zehlendorf is one of the most atmospheric and architecturally fascinating squares in Berlin. It is flanked by elegant semicircular Jugendstil apartment blocks, and in front of these stands Berlin's last remaining Art Deco-S-Bahn station. In summer, the buildings' balconies are decked with greenery and flowers. Some of Berlin's most magnificent mansion houses line Argentinische and Lindenthaler allees, the streets leading into the magnificent square.

10 Strandbad Wannsee

🏠 Wannseebadeweg 25
📞 (030) 803 54 50 ⏰ Hours vary, call to chech 🔗

Europe's largest inland beach (p67), which is almost 2 km (1 mile) long and 80 m (262 ft) wide, is a picturesque spot on the edge of the city. It is covered with sand from the Baltic. The swimming baths were built in 1929–30 as a recreation area for workers. Visitors can enjoy sports activities such as beach volleyball and football here.

A DAY IN THE SOUTHWEST

Morning

Start your walk through Berlin's southwestern districts by taking the S-Bahn (line S1) to **Mexikoplatz**. Admire the lovely villas and the green square before dropping in at **Café Krone** (No 2 Argentinische Allee) for a late breakfast. Then take bus No. 118 southwards to the open-air museum **Museumsdorf Düppel**. From there, take bus No. 115 north to the **Alliertenmuseum**. Afterwards, a 20-minute walk through the park opposite leads right up to the beer garden **Luise** (p157) near Freie Universität, where you can have lunch.

Afternoon

Stop at the **Museum Europäischer Kulturen** (p153), a two-minute walk south of the café, or discover tropical flora in the giant greenhouses of the **Botanischer Garten** (p66), a 20-minute walk east. The seasonal displays are spectacular. Then find your way to the Botanischer Garten S-Bahn station to take the train to the Wannsee station, gateway to the sights of southwestern Berlin. Head to the beaches of **Strandbad Wannsee**. Alternatively, visit the **Haus der Wannsee-Konferenz** and then admire the park. Finally, hop on the bus for an early dinner at **Luther & Wegner Schloß Glienicke** (p157). Your best option for returning to the centre is the S-Bahn from Wannsee.

The Best of the Rest

1. Open Air Museum Domäne Dahlem

🅰 Königin-Luise-Str. 49 🕒 Museum: 10am–5pm Sat & Sun; grounds: 7am–10pm daily 🔲 domaene-dahlem.de ☑

Learn about modern organic farming at this historic working farm.

2. Grunewaldturm

🅰 Havelchaussee 🕒 10am–10pm daily

This Neo-Gothic brick tower was built in 1897 as a memorial to Kaiser Wilhelm I. There is also a viewing platform on top.

3. Onkel Toms Hütte

🅰 Argentinische Allee

The "Uncle Tom's Hut" settlement, developed in 1926–32 according to designs by Bruno Taut and others, was intended to create a modern housing estate for workers.

4. Freie Universität

🅰 Habelschwerdter Allee 45 🕒 Library: 9am–10pm Mon–Fri, 9am–5pm Sat & Sun 🔲 fu-berlin.de

Berlin's largest university was founded in 1948 as a rival to the Humboldt University in East Berlin. It is worth looking at the 1950s Henry-Ford-Bau here, and the Philological Library, designed by Lord Norman Foster.

A beautiful garden at the Liebermann-Villa

5. Teufelsberg

🕒 11am–sunset Wed–Sun ☑

Situated on top of a hill, this Cold War-era listening tower is a landmark viewpoint. The surrounding forests are popular for biking and the Teufelsee lake for swimming and sunbathing (nude if you wish).

6. Heinrich von Kleist's Grave

🅰 Bismarckstr. 3, Am Kleinen Wannsee

German playwright Kleist and his companion Henriette Vogel committed suicide by shooting themselves in 1811; they are buried here together (near the S-Bahn overpass).

7. St-Peter-und-Paul-Kirche

🅰 Nikolshoer Weg 17 🕒 11am–4pm daily 🔲 kirche-nikolshoe.de

This stone church on the Havel was built in 1834–7 by Stüler and resembles Russian Orthodox churches.

8. Blockhaus Nikolskoe

🅰 Nikolshoer Weg 15 🕒 Noon–6pm daily

This wooden, Russian-style *dacha*, built in 1819, was a gift from King Friedrich Wilhelm III to his daughter Charlotte and his son-in-law, the future Tsar Nicholas I.

9. St-Annen-Kirche

🅰 Königin-Luise-Str./Pacelliallee

This 14th-century Gothic church has attractive murals depicting scenes from the life of St Anna, as well as late Gothic figures of saints and a Baroque pulpit.

10. Liebermann-Villa

🅰 Colomierstr. 3 🕒 Summer: 10am–6pm Wed–Mon; winter: 11am–5pm Wed–Mon 🔲 liebermann-villa.de

The home of Berlin painter Max Liebermann, on the Wannsee shore, is now a museum of his art.

Restaurants

PRICE CATEGORIES

For a three-course meal for one with half a bottle of wine (or equivalent meal), taxes and charges included.

€ under €30 €€ €30–60 €€€ over €60

1. Mutter Fourage

⬛ Chausseestrasse 15a ⏰ Summer: 9am–7pm daily; winter: 10am–6pm daily 🌐 mutterfourage.de · €

Hidden in the yard of a market garden and an atelier, this charming café has a delicious selection of homemade cakes and snacks.

2. Haus Sanssouci

⬛ Am Großen Wannsee 60 ⏰ 11:30am–11pm Tue–Sun 🌐 web.haussanssouci.com · €€

Offering great views of Wannsee, this idyllic cottage-style restaurant serves up mostly German food, but it has lobster nights and other specials too.

3. Floh

⬛ Am Bahnhof Grunewald 4 ⏰ Noon–11pm daily 🌐 restaurant-floh.business.site · €

A rustic pub, Floh (Flea) is known for its homemade dishes. Its beer garden is right next to the Grundewald S-Bahn station.

4. La Gondola Due

⬛ Mexikoplatz 4 ⏰ 5pm–midnight Tue–Sat, noon–10pm Sun 🌐 lagondoladue.de · €€

This wonderful Italian restaurant is known for its great pastas, excellent wines and fantastic service.

5. Alter Krug Dahlem

⬛ Königin-Luise-Str. 52 ⏰ 10am–midnight daily 🌐 alter-krug-berlin.de · €

Relax in the porch swings of this large beer garden. A barbecue provides the food at mealtimes.

Outdoor setting at the Alter Krug Dahlem

6. Blockhaus Nikolskoe

⬛ Nikolskoer Weg 15 ⏰ Noon–6pm daily 🌐 blockhaus-nikolskoe.de · €€

Traditional German fare is on offer at this historic cabin with a water view.

7. Luise

⬛ Königin-Luise-Str. 40 ⏰ 11am–11pm Mon–Thu, 11am–midnight Fri, 10am–midnight Sat, 10am–11pm Sun 🌐 luise-dahlem.de · €

On the Freie Universität campus, Luise always has a good atmosphere. Try the great salads and sandwiches.

8. Café Max

⬛ Villa Liebermann, Colomierstr. 3 ⏰ Apr–Sep: 10am–6pm Wed–Mon; Oct–Mar: 11am–5pm Wed–Mon 🌐 cafe-max-liebermann.de · €€

The café in the museum of the famous painter Max Liebermann has a lovely garden and lake views. Access to the café is with museum admission.

9. Luther & Wegner Schloß Glienicke

⬛ Königstr. 36 ⏰ Noon–9pm Wed–Sun 🌐 schloss-glienicke.de · €€

Sophisticated surroundings and cuisine. Fish dishes and salads in summer, game and roasts in winter.

10. Chalet Suisse

⬛ Clayallee 99 ⏰ Noon–midnight daily 🌐 chalet-suisse.de · €€

Enjoy local and Swiss cooking in a cosy atmosphere at Chalet Suisse.

POTSDAM AND SANSSOUCI

Potsdam is an important part of European cultural history – a splendid centre of the Enlightenment, which reached its climax in the 18th century in the architectural and artistic design of Frederick the Great's palace of Sanssouci. The palace complex, with its beautiful, extensive park, is both magnificent and playful. It has been designated a World Heritage Centre of Culture by UNESCO and enchants millions of visitors every year. The town of Potsdam, with more than 150,000 inhabitants, is the capital of the federal province of Brandenburg. This former garrison town has much to delight visitors, including small palaces and old churches, idyllic parks and historic immigrant settlements.

1 Top 10 Sights
p159

1 Restaurants
p163

1 The Best of the Rest
p162

For places to stay in this area, see p177

The decadent Baroque Neues Palais in Park Sanssouci

1 Neues Palais

📍 Am Neuen Palais 🕐 10am–6pm
Wed–Mon (Nov–Mar: to 5pm)
🌐 spsg.de ♿🅿️

One of Germany's most beautiful
palaces, the Baroque Neues Palais was
built in 1763–9 for Frederick the Great by
Johann Gottfried Büring, Jean Laurent
Le Geay and Carl von Gontard. The vast
structure has 200 rooms, including
the Marmorsaal (marble hall), a lavish
ballroom, and the Schlosstheater,
where plays are once more performed
today. Frederick's private chambers are
equally splendid, especially his Rococo
study, the upper gallery with valuable
parquet flooring and the Oberes
Vestibül, a room clad in marble.

2 Museum Barberini

📍 Alter Markt, Humboldtstr. 5–6
🕐 11am–7pm Tue–Sun 🌐 museum-
barberini.com ♿

This private art museum, once Palace
Barberini, was built in 1771–72 by
Frederick the Great. Destroyed during
the war, it was reconstructed by Hasso
Plattner, and opened to the public in
2017. The rooms house 250 paintings
and sculptures from Plattner's
collection and others on loan.

3 Schloss Sanssouci

📍 Maulbeerallee 🕐 For tours only;
Apr–Oct: 10am–6pm Tue–Sun (Nov–
Mar: to 5pm) 🌐 spsg.de ♿🅿️

Frederick the Great wished to live
"sans souci" (without worries) in a
palace outside the city. In 1745, he
commissioned architect Georg
Wenzeslaus von Knobelsdorff to
construct this Rococo palace using
his own designs. The structure has
a marble hall at the centre of the
complex and pays homage to Rome's
Pantheon. To its left and right are
rooms designed by Johann August Nahl
and von Knobelsdorff; these include
the concert room and the king's library.
Here, the monarch liked to play the
flute or to philosophize with Voltaire.
Works by Antoine Watteau adorn the
palace walls.

Schloss Cecilienhof, with a pretty herringbone pattern on its exterior

4 Schloss Cecilienhof

🏛 Im Neuen Garten ⏰ Apr–Oct: 10am–6pm Tue–Sun (Nov–Mar: to 5pm) 🌐 spsg.de

The 1945 Potsdam Conference was held in this palace, built in 1914–17 in the style of an English country house. Now a UNESCO World Heritage Site, it houses a hotel and a small exhibition.

5 Schloss Charlottenhof

🏛 Geschwister-Scholl-Str. 34a ⏰ May–Oct: 10am–6pm Tue–Sun 🌐 spsg.de

A Neo-Classical palace in Park Sanssouci, the Schloss Charlottenhof was built in 1829 by Schinkel for Friedrich Wilhelm IV. Particularly worth seeing here is the tent-like Humboldtsaal.

6 Schlosspark Sanssouci

🏛 Maulbeerallee ⏰ Hours vary, check website 🌐 spsg.de

It is easy to spend a day in a park as large as this one. Among the many charming buildings hidden in the landscaped garden is the Rococo-style Chinesisches Haus (Am Grünen Gitter), built in 1754–6 by Johann Gottfried Büring. It originally served as a teahouse and dining room, and now houses an exhibition of East Asian porcelain. The Römische Bäder (Lennéstr), or Roman Baths, are lakeside pavilions modelled on an Italian Renaissance villa. They were built as bath- and guesthouses between 1829 and 1840 by Schinkel. The Orangerie (An der Orangerie 3–5), built in 1851–60 by Stüler, was also originally intended for the king's guests. Today it houses a small gallery of paintings.

7 Holländisches Viertel

🏛 Friedrich-Ebert-, Kurfürsten-, Hebbel-, Gutenbergstr.

A pleasant way to explore Potsdam is a walk through the historic Old Town. Built between 1733 and 1742, the area originally served as a settlement for Dutch workers, after whom it is now named.

THE POTSDAM CONFERENCE

In July and August 1945, the heads of the governments of the United States (Harry Truman), the USSR (Joseph Stalin) and Great Britain (Winston Churchill) met in Schloss Cecilienhof in order to seal the future of Germany through a treaty. Vitally important points, such as the level of reparations to be paid by Germany, the demilitarization of the country, its new borders, the punishment of war criminals, and the resettlement of Germans from Poland were decided here.

Interior of the Neo-Classical Nikolaikirche with its vast dome

8 Marmorpalais
🏛Heiliger See (Neuer Garten)
🕐May–Oct: 10am–6pm Tue–Sun;
Nov–Apr: 10am–4pm Sat & Sun
🌐spsg.de

This small, early Neo-Classical palace by the Heiliger See was built in 1791–7 by architect Carl Gotthard Langhans and others. It features an elegant concert hall as well as contemporary furniture and porcelain.

9 Marstall (Filmmuseum)
🏛Breite Str. 1a 🕐10am–6pm
Tue–Sun 🌐filmmuseum-pots
dam.de

Set in the Baroque former stable buildings of the king's town residence, this small museum uses old cameras, props and projectors to document the history of German film.

10 Nikolaikirche
🏛Am Alten Markt 🕐9am–6pm
Mon–Sat, 11:30am–5pm Sun

Potsdam's most attractive church, Nikolaikirche was designed by Schinkel in 1830 in Neo-Classical style. Its giant dome is particularly striking, and you can ascend it for a view over the Stadtschloss, which is now home to the parliament of Brandenburg.

A DAY IN POTSDAM

Morning
Begin your exploration in the Schlosspark Sanssouci as early as possible in order to get ahead of the daily influx of visitors. Start with **Schloss Sanssouci** (p159) and **Neues Palais** then visit the Chinesisches Haus, Römische Bäder and Orangerie. From Schlosspark walk along Voltaireweg to Neuer Garten in the northeast of Potsdam, where you can recover over a tasty lunch at **Brauerei Meierei** (Im Neuen Garten 10).

Afternoon
Start the afternoon at **Schloss Cecilienhof** and stroll through Neuer Garten. Stop for a break at Heiliger See, then head to the centre of Potsdam, starting with the **Holländisches Viertel** (Dutch quarter) where you could pop into one of the numerous cafés. Stroll past the St Peter-und-Paul Kirche (p162), the Französische Kirche (p162), the **Nikolaikirche** and the **Altes Rathaus** (p162) to the **Marstall** film museum and Museum Barberini. If you have time, extend your tour by driving to nearby Babelsberg. You could either visit the Filmpark (p162), admire Schloss Babelsberg or walk up Telegrafenberg. Round off your day with a delicious meal at **Pino** (p163) in Potsdam.

The Best of the Rest

Brandenburger Tor, one of Potsdam's famous gates

1. Alexandrowka
⌂ Russische Kolonie/Puschkinallee
The Russian colony feels like a village in Tsarist Russia. Decorated log cabins with gardens were built here in 1826 for a Russian military choir. Don't miss the museum and the Alexander Newski church.

2. Dampfmaschinenhaus
⏱ Breite Str. 28 ⏱ May–Oct: 10am–6pm Sat & Sun 🌐 spsg.de
This building, resembling a mosque with minarets, is the water pumping station for Sanssouci. The 1842 pump can be seen inside.

3. Telegrafenberg
⌂ Albert-Einstein-Str. 🔲🔲
The Einstein tower on top of Telegraph Hill was designed by Erich Mendelsohn in 1920. Einsteinturm tours organizes guided trips from October to March.

4. Schloss Babelsberg
⌂ Park Babelsberg ⏱ For renovation until 2025 🌐 spsg.de
Built by Schinkel, this Neo-Gothic building sits in an idyllic park on the banks of the Havel River. The building is closed for renovation, but the park is open to visitors. Check the website for details of temporary exhibitions.

5. Potsdamer Stadtschloss
⌂ Neuer Markt
The Hohenzollern palace, once the residence of Frederick the Great, was badly bombed in World War II and had to be demolished in 1960. It is the cultural centre and the seat of the Potsdam legislative assembly.

6. Altes Rathaus
⌂ Am Alten Markt
The old town hall, built in 1753, is decorated with sculptures and Potsdam's coat of arms – two gilded Atlas figures, each carrying a globe on its back. Today, it is home to the town's museum.

7. Filmpark Babelsberg
⌂ Großbeerenstr. 200, Potsdam ⏱ Late Mar–early Nov: 10am–6pm daily ⏱ For events/event days, check website 🌐 filmpark-babelsberg.de 🔲
The Filmpark *(p70)* offers visitors a tour of the legendary UFA-Studios, complete with U-boat trips and stunt performances.

8. Französische Kirche
⌂ Am Bassinplatz 📞 (0331) 29 12 19 ⏱ Late Mar–mid-Oct: 1:30–5pm Tue–Sun
In 1752, Johann Boumann built this elliptical Huguenot church with its columned portico; Schinkel designed the beautiful interior in the 1830s.

9. St-Peter-und-Paul-Kirche
⌂ Am Bassinplatz 📞 (0331) 230 79 90 ⏱ 10am–6pm daily (winter: to 5pm)
Based on Haghia Sophia in Istanbul, the Catholic church of St Peter and St Paul was built in 1867–70 by Stüler.

10. Brandenburger Tor
⌂ Luisenplatz
The most attractive of Potsdam's five former town gates was built by Gontard and Unger in 1770 to celebrate Prussian victory in the Seven Years' War.

Restaurants

1. Kades am Pfingstberg
🏠 Große Weinmeisterstr. 43b
🕐 Noon–3pm & 5–9pm Thu–Mon
🌐 restaurant-pfingstberg.de · €€
This spot features an outdoor terrace overlooked by lush trees, as well as an open fireplace inside. Wherever you sit, enjoy local dishes like venison goulash.

2. Zanotto
🏠 Dortustr. 53 🕐 6–10pm Wed–Sun
🌐 daszanottopotsdam.de · €€
This Italian restaurant uses fresh seasonal ingredients and home-made pasta.

3. Pino
🏠 Weinbergstr. 7 🕐 6pm–midnight Mon–Sat 🌐 pino-potsdam.de · €€
Close to Park Sanssouci, Pino serves a daily changing menu of exquisite Sicilian fare. The wine list reads like a Who's Who of Italian vintages.

4. Restaurant Juliette
🏠 Jägerstr. 39 🕐 5–10pm Wed–Sun, also noon–2:30pm Sat & Sun
🗓 Jul 🌐 restaurant-juliette.de · €€
Set in a former manor house this charming restaurant serves top-quality French classics.

5. Otto Hiemke
🏠 Karl-Gruhl-Str. 55 🕐 4–11pm daily (from noon Fri–Sun) · €
This welcoming pub has been family-run since 1896, and offers a traditional German menu.

vintage Ford vehicle used by the Café Heider for advertising

6. Maison Charlotte
🏠 Mittelstr. 20 🕐 Noon–10pm daily
🌐 maison-charlotte.de · €€
An old-world wine bar in a red-brick Dutch house with outdoor seating in a pleasant courtyard, Maison Charlotte serves French country fare and fine wines.

7. Villa Kellermann
🏠 Mangerstr. 34 🕐 6–11pm Wed–Fri, noon–4:30pm & 6–11pm Sat
🌐 villakellermann.de · €€€
This elegant Michelin-starred restaurant by Heiliger See features uniquely designed rooms. Locals come here to enjoy traditional German cuisine with a modern twist.

8. Waage
🏠 Am Neuen Markt 12 🕐 4–11pm Tue–Sat, noon–10pm Sun 🌐 restaurant-waage.de · €€
The regional meat and fish dishes at this attractive historic restaurant in central Potsdam are particularly worth trying.

9. Café Heider
🏠 Friedrich-Ebert-Str. 29 🕐 9am–10pm daily 🌐 cafeheider.de · €
This lovely café in the middle of Potsdam's Old Town offers a fantastic breakfast, which you can enjoy outside on the terrace in summer.

10. La Madeleine
🏠 Lindenstr. 9 🕐 Noon–10pm daily
🌐 creperie-potsdam.de · €
A little bistro serving all sorts of crêpes, such as sweet with jam or savoury with ham – the ideal spot for a quick snack.

STREETSMART

Bagel seller cycling through the

GETTING AROUND

Whether exploring Berlin by foot or public transport, and for a short city break or a longer stay, here is everything you need to know to navigate the city and its surrounding areas like a pro.

SPEED LIMIT

MOTORWAY	REGIONAL ROADS
130 km/h (80 mph)	**100** km/h (60 mph)

RURAL ROADS	URBAN AREAS
70 km/h (40 mph)	**50** km/h (30 mph)

Arriving by Air

Berlin's two international airports, Tegel (TXL) and Schönefeld (SXF), were replaced in October 2020 by a new regional hub, the long-awaited **Berlin-Brandenburg (BER)**. Situated some 18 km (11 miles) southeast of the city on the former sight of Schönefeld airport, Berlin-Brandenburg is very well connected and receives regular flights from Europe, North America and Asia. Schönefeld now operates as Brandenburg's fifth terminal.

The fastest way to travel to and from the airport is the S-Bahn commuter train RE7 or RB14, or the FEX Airport Express, direct to Berlin Hauptbahnhof in 30 minutes. Regular city buses link the airport to the U-Bahn network.
Berlin-Brandenburg (BER)
W berlin-airport.de

International Train Travel

International high-speed trains connect Berlin to other cities across Europe. Reservations are essential.

You can buy tickets and passes for mutiple international train journeys from **Eurail** or **Interrail**. Depending on the service, an additional reservation fee may apply. Always check that your pass is valid on the service you wish to travel with before boarding; travelling without reservations can incur a fine.

Eurostar runs a regular service from London, via the Channel Tunnel, to Brussels, where you can change for Berlin. **Deutsche Bahn**, Germany's national rail network, also runs a regular high-speed service to and from other European destinations.

Students and those under the age of 26 can benefit from discounted rail travel both to and in Germany. For more information on discounts, visit the Eurail or Interrail websites.
Deutsche Bahn
W bahn.com
Eurail
W eurail.com

Eurostar

W eurostar.com

Interrail

W interrail.eu

Long-Distance Bus Travel

Eurolines offers a variety of coach routes to Berlin from other European cities. Fares start from £19, with discounts for students, children and seniors. Other services include **FlixBus**, **Student Agency Bus** and **Ecolines**.

The **Zentraler Omnibus Bahnhof (ZOB)** is the city's largest long-distance bus station, with connections to towns all over Germany and the rest of Europe. Check online for timetables and tickets.

Ecolines

W ecolines.net

Eurolines

W eurolines.com

FlixBus

W flixbus.de

Student Agency Bus

W studentagencybus.com

Zentraler Omnibus Bahnhof (ZOB)

W zob-berlin.de

Public Transport

Berliner Verkehrsbetriebe (BVG) is Berlin's main public transport authority and service provider. Safety and hygiene measures, timetables, ticket information and transport maps can be found online.

BVG

W bvg.de

Tickets

Berlin is divided into three travel zones for the purposes of ticket pricing: A, B and C. Zone A covers the city centre,

Zone B the outskirts of town and Zone C includes Berlin's suburban areas, Potsdam and its environs, as well as Berlin-Brandeburg airport. Tickets for any combination of zones are available and are valid on all forms of public transport, including trains, trams, S-Bahn, U-Bahn and ferries, for two hours, with unlimited changes.

Travel is only valid in one direction, so a second ticket is required for the return journey. Short-trip (*kurzstrecke*) tickets are cheaper, but can only be used for three stops on trains and six stops on buses and trams. Daily (*tageskarte*) and seven-day tickets (*24-stunden-karte*), costing €8.80 and €36 respectively for zones A–B, are better value if you are making multiple journeys. Seven-day tickets also allow you to travel with one extra adult or up to three children for free after 8pm, on weekends and on public holidays.

Discounted tickets are available with tourist cards that offer combined public transport and museum entry (*p173*).

Ticket machines at train stations and on board trams accept cash only. Exact change is required on buses. Tickets must be validated in the red or yellow time-stamping machine at platform entrances or on board buses. If caught without a valid ticket you face a fine.

Regional and Local Trains

Germany's railways are operated by Deutsche Bahn (DB). Regional Bahn and Regional Express (RB and RE) trains service the wider Berlin-Brandenburg region and beyond. Use this service for day trips to Potsdam and other towns near Berlin.

GETTING TO AND FROM BERLIN BRANDENBURG

Transport to city centre	Journey Time	Price
Airport Express (FEX)	25 mins	€3.80
RE7	30 mins	€3.80
RB14	30 mins	€3.80
S-Bahn (S9/S45)	50 mins	€3.80
Taxi	40 mins	€60

U-Bahn and S-Bahn

Don't let the name confuse you: Berlin's "underground" trains also run on elevated tracks above ground. There are 10 U-Bahn lines, each connecting with the S-Bahn and other U-Bahn lines at points across Berlin. The service usually closes between 12:30am and 4am. On weekends all lines are open 24 hours except the U4 and U55. U-Bahn stations are marked by a rectangular blue sign with a large, white letter U.

The S-Bahn is faster than the U-Bahn, and its stations are further apart from one another. Berlin has 16 S-Bahn lines in total, running well beyond the confines of the city. Trains run every 10 or 20 minutes, or more frequently during peak travel times. S-Bahn stations are marked by a round, green sign, featuring a large, white letter S.

Buses

Several bus services operate in Berlin, and they all use the same ticket tariffs. City buses are marked by three-digit route codes and operate every 20 minutes between 5am and midnight. Major routes are serviced by Metro buses (marked by a letter M before the route number), operating 24 hours, and running every 10 to 20 minutes, while express buses (marked by a letter X) run every 5 to 20 minutes.

The night bus service operates every half an hour from midnight until 4am, when the U-Bahn service resumes. Regular tickets are not valid on this service. Night bus tickets can be bought from the driver (cash only).

All bus routes have a detailed timetable on display at each stop, and inner-city bus stops are equipped with digital screens indicating waiting times. Consult the BVG website (p167) for specific route information.

Trams

Despite only servicing the eastern parts of the city, trams (strassenbahn) are a popular way to get around, particularly if you are travelling from Mitte to any part of Prenzlauer Berg. Important routes are serviced by Metro trams running every 10 or 20 minutes, 24 hours a day. Some run a reduced service on weekends. Other tram services run every 20 minutes between 5 or 6am and midnight.

Public Ferries

An extensive system of canals and lakes links the city centre with neighbouring Potsdam, Spandau, Charlottenburg and Müggelsee, making boating not only a fun way to see the sights but also a viable way to get around.

Six ferry lines operate in Berlin as part of the city's integrated public transport system. Marked by a letter F, they provide cross-river connections in locations to the east of the centre.

Taxis

Official Berlin taxis are cream, have a "Taxi" sign on the roof and have a meter on the driver's dashboard. Taxi apps such as Uber and Lyft also operate.

Taxis can be hailed on the street, picked up at taxi ranks (würfelfunk) or booked in advance online or over the phone from firms such as **Taxi Funk Berlin** or **Würfelfunk**. If you are travelling 2 km (1 mile) or less, ask for a short trip (kurzstrecke) for €5 – this can only be requested in taxis that you have hailed on the street.

Taxi Funk Berlin
W funk-taxi-berlin.de
Würfelfunk
W wuerfelfunk.de

Driving

Berlin is easily reached by car from most European cities via E-roads, which form the International European Road Network. Germany's regional roads (landesstrassen) are marked with yellow road signs, while motorways (autobahnen) are marked with blue road signs. Some stretches of motorway have variable speed limits depending on weather and road conditions; others have no enforced speed limit.

erman drivers therefore tend to zoom
long at high speeds.

Drivers must carry their passport
nd insurance documentation if driving
foreign-registered vehicle. Driving
cences issued by any of the EU
nember states are valid. If visiting
rom outside the EU, you may need
o apply for an International Driving
ermit. Check with your local auto-
mobile association before you travel.

You must be 21 or over and have
eld a valid driving licence for at least
year to rent a car in Germany. By law,
rivers aged 21–22 must buy a Collision
Damage Waiver (CDW). Drivers under
5 may incur a young-driver surcharge.

In the event of a breakdown or
ccident, or if you require assistance,
ontact **ADAC Auto Assistance**.

Berlin is surrounded by a circular
notorway called the Berliner Ring,
vhich has numerous signposted exits
hat lead straight to the city centre.
Vhile public transport is the easiest
vay to get around, Berlin is relatively
traightforward to navigate by car;
oad layouts are clear and streets are
vell signposted. Parking is not hard to
nd and is relatively cheap. Always
rive on the right. Unless otherwise
ignposted, vehicles coming from the
ight always have priority. Beware of
yclists and trams; trams take prece-
ence, so take care when turning, and
llow cyclists right of way. Seatbelts
re compulsory in a hired car, lights
nust be used in tunnels and the use of
mobile phone while driving is
rohibited. The drink-drive *(p173)* limit
strictly enforced.

All drivers must have third-party
nsurance. Also compulsory is an
nvironmental badge for vehicles
riving within environmental green
ones known as **Umweltzonen**. Most
f downtown Berlin is an Umweltzone.
ertification can be purchased online.

DAC Auto Assistance
adac.de

mweltzonen
umwelt-plakette.de

Cycling

Berlin is generally a very bike-friendly
city, with many designated cycle lanes
and traffic lights at intersections. If you
get tired of pedalling, bikes can be
taken on the U-Bahn, S-Bahn and trams
(with an additional bicycle ticket), but
they are prohibited on buses, except
night buses, which can carry up to two
at the driver's discretion.

Deutsche Bahn (DB) operates an
excellent public bicycle system called
LIDL Bike. Bikes can be picked up from
train stations and major intersections,
and dropped off at any of the LIDL Bike
stations around the city. To rent a LIDL
Bike, register by providing your credit
card details. A one-off registration fee
of €3 applies. The first 30 minutes cost
€1.50, and you will be charged €1 for
every additional half hour. You can also
hire bikes at cycling shops for similar or
cheaper rates; one of the most reliable
is **Fahrradstation**. Be aware that drink-
drive limits also apply to cyclists.

Cyclists should ride on the right. If in
doubt, dismount: many cyclists cross
junctions on foot; if you do so, switch to
the pedestrian section of the crossing.
Beware of tram tracks; try to cross
them at an angle to avoid getting the
wheels stuck. For your own safety, do
not walk with your bike in a bike lane or
cycle on pavements, on the left side of
the road, in designated pedestrian
zones or in the dark without lights. The
locals usually don't bother, but wearing
a helmet is highly recommended.

Fahrradstation
w fahrradstation.com

LIDL Bike
w lidl-bike.de

Walking

Berlin is one of the largest cities in
Europe, but is still pleasantly walkable.
Most of the major sights are located
within a relatively small, mostly
walkable area. Organized walking tours
are also a popular option for those
looking to explore the city on foot
and learn its history along the way.

PRACTICAL INFORMATION

A little local know-how goes a long way in Berlin. On these pages you can find all the essential advice and information you will need to make the most of your trip to the city.

AT A GLANCE

CURRENCY
Euro (EUR)

AVERAGE DAILY SPEND

SAVE
€60

SPEND
€125

SPLURGE
€200+

BOTTLED WATER
€1.30

COFFEE
€2.50

BEER
€3.50

DINNER FOR TWO
€65

ESSENTIAL PHRASES

Hello	Guten Tag
Goodbye	Auf Wiedersehen
Please	Bitte
Thank you	Danke
Do you speak English?	Sprechen Sie Englisch?
I don't understand	Ich verstehe nicht

ELECTRICITY SUPPLY

Power sockets are type F and L, fitting two-pronged plugs. Standard voltage is 230 volts.

Passports and Visas

For entry requirements, including visas, consult your nearest German embassy or check the **German Federal Foreign Office** website. Citizens of the UK, US, Canada, Australia and New Zealand do not need a visa for stays of up to three months, but in future must apply in advance for the European Travel Information and Authorization System (**ETIAS**); roll-out has continuall been postponed so check the website for details. EU nationals do not need a visa or an ETIAS.

ETIAS
W travel-europe.europa.eu/etias_en
German Federal Foreign Office
W auswaertiges-amt.de

Government Advice

Now more than ever, it is important to consult both your and the German government's advice before travelling. The UK Foreign, Commonwealth and Development Office (**FCDO**), the **US Department of State**, the **Australian Department of Foreign Affairs and Trade** and the German Federal Foreign Office offer the latest information on security, health and local regulations.

Australian Department of Foreign Affairs and Trade
W smartraveller.gov.au
UK FCDO
W gov.uk/foreign-travel-advice
US Department of State
W travel.state.gov

Customs Information

You can find information on the laws relating to goods and currency taken in or out of Germany on the **Zoll** (Federal Customs Service) website.
W zoll.de

Insurance

We recommend taking out a comprehensive insurance policy covering theft, loss of belongings, medical care, cancellations and delays, and read the small print carefully.

UK citizens are eligible for free emergency medical care in Germany, provided they have a valid European Health Insurance Card (EHIC) or UK Global Health Insurance Card (**GHIC**).

GHIC

🆆 ghic.org.uk

Vaccinations

No inoculations are needed for Berlin.

Money

Major credit, debit and prepaid currency cards are widely accepted. Contactless payments are becoming the norm, too, though they are still not used on public transport, so it is always worth carrying some cash on you. Cash machines are located at various points throughout the city centre.

Tipping is not expected in Berlin, but it is common to add a tip of 5–10 per cent in restaurants if the service is good.

Travellers with Specific Requirements

Berlin is well-equipped for visitors with mobility requirements. Pavements are sloped at junctions and most public buildings, malls and cinemas are fitted with lifts, ramps and extra-wide doors. The **German Red Cross (DRK)** rents out wheelchairs.

S- and U-Bahn trains are wheelchair accessible, but not all stations have lifts. If you are in the U-Bahn, wait at the head of the platform, and the driver will put up a ramp. In the S-Bahn, speak to the station manager to have a ramp set up. BVG maps show all of the accessible stations. Buses with a wheelchair symbol have a ramp. Download the free **accessBerlin** app (p172) for details of the most accessible routes around the city.

Berlin's charitable association for the blind and sight-impaired, the **Allgemeiner Blinden-und Sehbehindertenverein**, offers practical advice and useful information.

Allgemeiner Blinden-und Sehbehindertenverein

🆆 absv.de

German Red Cross (DRK)

🆆 drk-berlin.de/reservierung.html

Language

German is the official language, but Berlin is a global city, and English is almost as prevalent as German. The majority of Berliners speak English, and you can easily get by in shops and restaurants without knowing a word of German, but it's always appreciated if you can handle a few niceties in the local language.

Opening Hours

On weekdays, small retailers generally open at 9am or 10am and shut by 7pm, while department stores close at 10pm. Large supermarkets open 8am–10pm. Most shutters go down at 4pm on Saturdays. Shops in large train stations and service stations and convenience stores (*spätkauf*) stay open until at least midnight, and are also open on Sundays.

Banks in the city centre work 9am–4pm Monday to Wednesday, till 6pm on Thursday, and till 2pm on Friday. Larger post offices work 8am–6pm Monday to Friday, and until at least noon on Saturday. Pharmacies open 9am–7pm Monday to Friday, and until 4pm on Saturday.

Public museums are generally open 10am–6pm; many close on Monday. On public holidays, schools, post offices and banks are closed for the day, and shops, museums and attractions either close early or are closed for the entire day.

Situations can change quickly and unexpectedly. Always check before visiting attractions and hospitality venues for up-to-date opening hours and booking requirements.

Personal Security

Berlin is a relatively safe city, but as in most cities, use common sense. Pick-pocketing is common, particularly at tourist sites. Contact your embassy if your passport has been stolen, or in the event of a serious crime or accident.

Germans, and Berliners in particular, are generally accepting of all people, regardless of their race, gender or sexuality. While long celebrated as a liberal and tolerant country, Germany only legalized homosexuality in 1994. Despite the freedoms that the LGBTQ+ community enjoy in Berlin, acceptance is not always a given. If you do feel unsafe, the **Safe Space Alliance** pinpoints your nearest place of refuge.

The **Maneo** hotline run by **Mann-O-Meter** supports victims of homophobic behaviour. **Lesbenberatung** is a lesbian safe space that offers help, advice and counselling for women and transgender people.

Lesbenberatung
🆆 lesbenberatung-berlin.de
Maneo
🆆 maneo.de
Mann-O-Meter
🆆 mann-o-meter.de
Safe Space Alliance
🆆 safespacealliance.com

Health

Berlin is known for its world-class health service. EU citizens can receive emergency medical treatment in Germany free of charge (p171), but you may have to pay upfront and claim on your insurance later. For visitors from outside the EU, payment of medical expenses is the patient's responsibility. It is therefore important to arrange good medical insurance (p170).

For minor ailments and prescriptions, go to a chemist or pharmacy (apotheken). After 8pm, the address of the nearest all-night pharmacy is posted on the door of each outlet, or can be easily obtained by checking the **Apothekerkammer** website.

Apothekerkammer
🆆 akberlin.de

Smoking, Alcohol and Drugs

Germany has a smoking ban in all public places, including bars, cafés, restaurants and hotels.

Possession of narcotics is strictly prohibited and could result in prosecution and a prison sentence.

Unless stated otherwise, it is permitted to drink alcohol on the streets and in public parks. A strict drink-drive limit of 0.05 per cent BAC (blood alcohol content) is enforced.

ID

Visitors are not required to carry ID, but in the event of a routine check you may be asked to show your passport. If you don't have it with you, the police may escort you to where your passport is kept so that you can show it to them.

Local Customs

Germany has very strict laws on hate speech and symbols linked to Hitler and Nazism. Disrespectful behaviour in public places can warrant a fine, or even prosecution. Be respectful when visiting Berlin's historical sights and monuments. Pay attention to signage indicating when photos aren't allowed and think carefully about how you compose your shots. Visitors have come under serious criticism for posting inappropriate photos taken in front of sites such as the Holocaust-Denkmal (p93) on social media, for example.

Dress respectfully when visiting churches, synagogues and other religious buildings.

Mobile Phones and Wi-fi

Visitors travelling to Berlin with EU tariffs will be able to use their devices abroad without being affected by data roaming charges; instead they will be charged the same rates for data, SMS and voice calls as they would pay at home. Visitors with non-EU tariffs are advised to sign up for an international usage plan to keep costs down.

Berlin has over 400 wireless internet hotspots, many of which are free. Cafés and restaurants are usually happy to permit the use of their Wi-Fi on the condition that you make a purchase.

Responsible Travel

In a city where zero-waste restaurants, flea markets and urban farms are the norm, it's no wonder Berlin is one of the world's most sustainable cities. Visitors can do their bit by cycling or walking around the city to reduce emissions, embracing locally and sustainably sourced cuisine, and using reusable water bottles and bags.

Post

German mail is efficient, reliable and fast. Buy stamps from a post office counter or vending machines.

Postboxes generally have two slots: *Postleitzahlen* (postal codes) 10000–169999 for addresses in Brandenburg and Berlin, and *Andere Postleitzahlen* (other postal codes) for destinations elsewhere in Germany and abroad.
Deutsche Post
W deutschepost.de

Taxes and Refunds

VAT is 19 per cent in Germany. Non-EU residents are entitled to a tax refund subject to conditions. In order to do this, you must request a tax receipt and export papers (*ausfuhrbescheinigung*) when you purchase your goods. When leaving the country, present these papers, along with the receipt and your ID, at customs to receive your refund.

Discount Cards

The **Berlin WelcomeCard** offers free entry to 30 major tourist attractions and discounted entry for nearly 200 more. It also includes unlimited access to the transport network while in Berlin.

With the **Berlin Pass**, visitors get free entry to over 60 attractions, tours and museums and the option of an integrated travel card.

Save up to 30 per cent on the city's top 10 tourist attractions and enjoy unlimited free travel on public transport with the **Berlin City Tour Card**.
Berlin City Tour Card
W citytourcard.com
Berlin Pass
W berlinpass.com
Berlin WelcomeCard
W berlin-welcomecard.de

PLACES TO STAY

From luxurious hotels that recall the Golden Twenties to arty spots that celebrate an underground spirit, Berlin's accommodation is as exciting as the city itself. The best area depends on what you're after. Here for the nightlife? Book into buzzy hotels in Kreuzberg and Friedrichshain. Want to be near the bucket list sights? Opt for central Berlin areas like Alexanderplatz.

Historic hotels are everywhere, but take the chance to explore the city's quirky side too, staying at an indoor camping site or 19th-century former jail.

PRICE CATEGORIES

For a standard double room per night (with breakfast if included), taxes and extra charges.

€ under €120
€€ €120–€250
€€€ over €250

Central Berlin: Unter den Linden

Hotel Luc, Autograph Collection

Q L4 **A** Charlottenstr. 50 **W** marriott.com · €€€

With its bold splashes of deep Prussian blue on the walls, sofas and vases, Hotel Luc is a time capsule of Prussian elegance. A stay here will have you eager to learn more about Prussia's legacy, such as why the potato is the unofficial mascot for Prussian Germany; scan the QR code in the lobby, next to a basket of potatoes no less, to find out.

Château Royal Berlin

Q K3 **A** Neustädtische Kirchstr. 3 **W** chateauroyal berlin.com/de · €€€

No design detail has been overlooked at this sophisticated hotel, where individually styled rooms and suites feature contemporary art and custom-made oak furniture. It's all very refined and proper,

but stuffy it's not; the cocktail bar and rooftop are hangout spots for the city's artists.

Hotel de Rome

Q K4 **A** Behrenstr. 37 **W** roccofortehotels.com · €€€

Five stars come at a price at Hotel de Rome – fitting, given it's set in a 19th-century former bank. Elegant marble columns and an iron staircase are reminders of the building's past life, while upgrades have been given to the former jewellery vault (now housing a pool) and the bank directors' office (today, historic suites).

Central Berlin: Scheunenviertel

Monbijou Hotel

Q J5 **A** Monbijoupl. 1 **W** monbijouhotel.com · €

This affordable spot is at its most inviting in Berlin's chilling winter months, when a crackling fireplace keeps things cosy in the bar and lounge. Visiting in the summer? Make the most

of the rooftop, with 360-degree views of Berlin to blow your sandals off.

The Circus Hotel

Q G2 **A** Rosenthaler Str. 1 **W** circus-berlin.de · €€

Yoga sessions, bike rentals, street art walking tours: this hotel will keep you busy from morning till night. When you're tired of all the action, take a break in the gorgeous garden courtyard or enjoy a beer at the Lost My Voice bar.

Gorki Apartments

Q G2 **A** Weinbergsweg 25 **W** gorkiapartments.com/en · €€€

The luxurious Gorki Apartments come with all the trimmings: rainforest showers, bathtubs kitchenettes and Dyson hairdryers. With your very own doorbell and letterbox, as well as flea market finds dotting the interiors, it'll feel like a home away from home (albeit one located off Rosenthaler Platz, surrounded by some of Berlin's best restaurants)

St Christopher's Inn Berlin Mitte
📍 J4 🏠 Ziegelstr. 28
🌐 st-christophers.co.uk/berlin · €

If you're less bothered about the room itself and more about who you're sharing it with, this hostel is for you. Socializing is the beating heart of St Christopher's Inn, where guests chat on the rooftop terrace into the early hours, nurse drinks at the sports bar and bond on free walking tours offered through reception.

Hotel Telegraphenamt
📍 J5 🏠 Monbijoustr. 11
🌐 telegraphenamt.com · €€€

Set in a building that was once the biggest postal hub in Germany, this is a hotel you'll want to message home about. It's minutes from Museumsinsel, features impressive Neo-Baroque interiors and overlooks Monbijou Park. What makes it so special, though, is its stunning restaurant, ROOT, where global dishes are served under a conservatory roof.

Central Berlin: Around Alexanderplatz

Radisson Collection Hotel, Berlin
📍 J6 🏠 Karl-Liebhnecht-Str. 3 🌐 radissonhotels.com · €€

The Spree-side Radisson gets lots of ticks: central Mitte location, proximity to major sights, dreamy river and Berliner Dom views, sleek rooms and friendly staff. After a day of sightseeing, you can even indulge at the spa.

Tiergarten and the Federal District

Motel One Berlin-Potsdamer Platz
📍 L3 🏠 Leipziger Str. 132
🌐 motel-one.com · €

Swap a night at the museum for a night at the mall with Motel One, located in the fabulous Mall of Berlin. It's not only budget-friendly (leaving you more money to shop with) but is also perfectly placed to tick off the city's key sights.

The Mandala Hotel
📍 L2 🏠 Potsdamer Str. 3
🌐 themandala.de/de · €

Looking for a peaceful getaway but still want to be in the thick of the action? The Mandala Hotel has got you covered. Though located on bustling Potsdamer Platz, it's a peaceful sanctuary inside, and has been known to host celebrities seeking the utmost privacy (the hot stone massages and the two Michelin-starred Facil only add to the attraction).

Arte Luise Kunsthotel
📍 J3 🏠 Luisenstr. 19
🌐 luise-berlin.com/en · €€

Known as a "gallery to stay overnight", this arty hotel is Berlin through and through. All 50 rooms have been individually designed by an artist, and there's even a gallery on-site that doubles as an event venue. Better yet, the location on Unter den Linden means you're never far from the city's iconic galleries and museums (not that you'll need them).

Lulu Guldsmeden Hotel
📍 L2 🏠 Potsdamer Str. 67
🌐 guldsmedenhotels.com/lulu-guldsmeden · €€

This hotel means business when it comes to sustainability. Bathroom products and bed linens are eco-friendly, the loft-style rooms incorporate natural materials such as bamboo, and organic food and drink options are Green Globe-certified. Even the *Guldsmeden* newspaper, which offers tips on the city, is eco-certified; read your copy in the peaceful garden courtyard.

SO/ Berlin Das Stue
📍 E4 🏠 Drakestr. 1 🌐 so-berlin-das-stue.com · €€€

There's something to keep everyone happy here. For the kids, it's the setting, with floor-to-ceiling windows overlooking the Tiergarten and a private entrance to the Berlin Zoo. For the adults, it's the interiors, complete with a handsome bar and stunning white marble staircase.

InterContinental Berlin

Q D4 **A** Budapester Str. 2 **W** ihg.com/intercontinent al/hotels/gb/en/berlin · €€€

The InterContinental has rolled out the red carpet over the decades, with everyone from George W Bush to Tom Hanks booking in. Follow suit and you're promised award-winning sustainable practices, a top-notch spa and a Michelin-starred restaurant with skyline views. If you don't spot a celeb, sipping a cocktail at the Marlene Bar (named after Berlin-born singer and actress Marlene Dietrich) is the next best thing.

Charlottenburg and Spandau

Max Brown Hotel Ku'damm

Q C6 **A** Uhlandstr. 49 **W** maxbrownhotels.com/ kudamm-berlin · €

It's the little things that make a hotel feel like home: comfy beds to curl up in, dinky teapots to make the perfect cuppa, record players to listen to a collection of vinyl. Add to that bread baked on-site daily and stylish shops and bars on your doorstep and you'll want to move in.

Hotel Bristol Berlin

Q C5 **A** Kurfürstendamm 27 **W** bristolberlin.com · €€

Hotel Bristol is a Berlin icon. The city's first new luxury hotel after World War II, it quickly became synonymous with the city's glitterati, hosting the likes of Alfred Hitchcock and Sophia Loren. It remains a glamorous spot today, in part thanks to its Ku'damm location and stunning indoor pool. The highlight? Having the famous Crêpes Suzette flambéed at your table at the Bristol Grill restaurant.

Wilmina Hotel

Q B4 **A** Kantstr. 79 **W** wilmina.com · €€

Spending the night in jail doesn't ordinarily make for a happy holiday, unless you're staying at Wilmina. A women's prison from 1896 to 1985, the space has been creatively transformed, with original cell doors leading into elegant guest rooms. Enjoy contemporary German dishes served at the on-site restaurant.

Provocateur Hotel

Q B5 **A** Brandenburgische Str. 21 **W** provocateur-hotel.com · €€

The spirit of the Golden Twenties is alive and well at the Provocateur. Velvet seating, a gold-accented bar and dark walls in the common areas set the scene for a seductive stay. The theme extends to the rooms, with chandeliers, plush red headboards and black-tiled bathrooms. Get to your suite via the gold lift, a fixture since 1911.

Sir Savigny Hotel

Q B4 **A** Kantstr. 144 **W** sirhotels.com/en/ savigny · €

If you struggle to sleep in a hotel bed, book into Sir Savigny. Beds here are the stuff of dreams, with crispy 300 thread count cotton linens and pillows and mattresses you can sink into. It's the perfect place to retreat to after a day of exploring.

Kreuzberg, Schöneberg and Neukölln

Hüttenpalast

A Hobrechtstr. 65/66 **W** huettenpalast.de · €

Rain ruining your camping plans? You need Hüttenpalast, the world's first indoor caravan site. Here, restored vintage caravans are decked out with kitschy touches like furniture made of wine boxes, and communal areas are dotted with "trees" that light up at night. You can opt for one of the six traditional hotel rooms, each with its own bathroom, but where's the fun in that?

Orania Berlin

Q L5 **A** Oranienstr. 40 **W** orania.berlin · €€

Ideally located for Kreuzberg's vibrant nightlife scene, Orania will get your nights off to a great start. Live music concerts are held by jazz, soul and pop artists in the bar-lounge, the perfect place to mingle before hitting the nearby clubs and bars. When the early hours roll round, comfortable beds await.

The Yard Hotel

L6 · Alexandrinenstr. 125 · hotel-theyard.berlin · €€

You wouldn't know that some of the city's top sights, from the Jewish Museum to Checkpoint Charlie, were only a few minutes' walk from here. This quiet Kreuzberg spot is a serene oasis with an emphasis on minimalism, natural light and greenery. If the earthy tones aren't calming enough, book into the wellness centre.

Prenzlauer Berg

Hotel Oderberger

G1 · Oderberger Str. 57 · hotel-oderberger.berlin · €€

This hotel occupies a beautifully renovated 19th-century public bathhouse and as you'd expect its pool is a highlight. But there's so much more to shout about, such as vegan breakfast options, organic products in the bathrooms and in-room beauty treatments.

Linnen

G1 · Eberswalder Str. 35 · linnenberlin.com · €€

Everything here is set up to feel like home. The reception area doubles as a cosy café, where the friendly owners welcome you warmly and offer tips for your stay. As for the lodgings, you can choose from six rooms,

plus apartments and studios, all stocked with organic toiletries.

Berlin's Southeast

Michelberger Hotel

Warschauer Str. 39-40 · michelbergerhotel.com/en · €

If you plan on partying at Berlin's best clubs, you'll be well positioned here in the heart of Friedrichshain. Set in a former factory, the space is as cool and stylish as its guests, who pass the time nursing a drink on the lobby's low sofas or reading a book from the communal shelves.

nhow

Stralauer Allee 3 · nh-hotels.com/en/hotel · €

Want an electric guitar delivered to your room? Or a bluetooth speaker before a big night out? Europe's first music hotel has got you sorted. This Spree-side spot is wacky and wonderful, dotted with hot pink decor, funky furniture and lifts that have their own individual playlists.

Grunewald and Dahlem

Schlosshotel Berlin by Patrick Hellmann

Brahmsstr. 10 · schlosshotelberlin.com · €€€

What do Josephine Baker, Paul McCartney and the Rolling Stones have in common? They

all stayed at this elegant Italian Renaissance hotel (although only one trashed valuable vases while here). Aside from its celebrity guestbook, Schlosshotel Berlin is loved for its easy access to Grunewald forest walking trails.

Potsdam and Sanssouci

Hotel Brandenburger Tor Potsdam

Brandenburger Str. 1 · hotel-brandenburger-tor.de/en · €€

As impressive as the restored 18th-century hotel building is, the location sells this spot – stay here and you'll be within touching distance of the city's historic gate, Sanssouci Palace and the Dutch Quarter. Admire the surroundings with an aperitivo on the streetside terrace.

The niu Amity

L3 · Leipziger Str. 1/ Bloch J · the.niu.de/hotels · €

If you're nostalgic for youthful days spent camping with friends, you'll love the niu Amity. Boy scout badges dot the walls, long breakfast tables invite guests to mingle and comfy chairs are set up around a cute indoor campfire. The hotel also rewards you for saving energy and water: opt out of having your room cleaned and you'll get a free drink at the bar. Cheers to that.

INDEX

Page numbers in **bold** refer to main entries.

PHRASE BOOK

In an Emergency

Where is the telephone?	Wo ist das Telefon?	voh ist duss tel-e-fone?
Help!	Hilfe!	hilf-uh
Please call a doctor	Bitte rufen Sie einen Arzt	bitt-uh roof'n zee ine-en artst
Please call the police	Bitte rufen Sie die Polizei	bitt-uh roof'n zee dee poli-tsy
Please call the fire brigade	Bitte rufen Sie die Feuerwehr	bitt-uh roof'n zee dee foyer-vayr
Stop!	Halt!	hult

Communication Essentials

Yes	Ja	yah
No	Nein	nine
Please	Bitte	bitt-uh
Thank you	Danke	dunk-uh
Excuse me	Verzeihung	fair-tsy-hoong
Hello	Guten Tag	goot-en tahk
Goodbye	Auf Wiedersehen	owf veed-er-zay-ern
Good evening	Guten Abend	goot'n-ahb'nt
Good night	Gute Nacht	goot-un nukht
Until tomorrow	Bis morgen	biss morg'n
See you	Tschüss	chooss
What is that?	Was ist das?	voss ist duss
Why?	Warum?	var-room
Where?	Wo?	voh
When?	Wann?	vunn
today	heute	hoyt-uh
tomorrow	morgen	morg'n
month	Monat	mohn-aht
night	Nacht	nukht
afternoon	Nachmittag	nahkh-mit-tahk
morning	Morgen	morg'n
year	Jahr	yar
there	dort	dort
here	hier	hear
week	Woche	vokh-uh
yesterday	gestern	gest'n
evening	Abend	ahb'nt

Useful Phrases

How are you? (informal)	Wie geht's?	vee gayts
Fine, thanks	Danke, es geht mir gut	dunk-uh, es gayt meer goot
Where is/are?	Wo ist/sind...?	voh ist/sind
How far is it to...?	Wie weit ist es...?	vee vite ist ess
Do you speak English?	Sprechen Sie Englisch?	shpresh'n zee eng-glish
I don't understand.	Ich verstehe nicht	ish fair-shtay-uh nisht
Could you speak more slowly?	Könnten Sie langsamer sprechen?	kurnt-en zee langsamer shpresh'n

Useful Words

large	gross	grohss
small	klein	kline
hot	heiss	hyce
cold	kalt	kult
good	gut	goot
bad	böse/schlecht	burss-uh/shlesht
open	geöffnet	g'urff-nett
closed	geschlossen	g'shloss'n
left	links	links
right	rechts	reshts
straight ahead	geradeaus	g'rah-der-owss

Making a Telephone Call

I would like to make a phone call	Ich möchte telefonieren	ish mer-shtuh tel-e-fon-eer'n
I'll try again later	Ich versuche noch ein mal später	ish fair-zookh-uh nokh ine-mull shpay-ter
Can I leave a message?	Kann ich eine Nachricht hinterlassen?	kan ish ine-uh nakh-risht hint-er-lahss-en
answer phone	Anrufbeantworter	an-roof-be-ahnt-vort-er
telephone card	Telefonkarte	tel-e-fohn-kart-uh
receiver	Hörer	hur-er
mobile	Handy	han-dee
engaged (busy)	besetzt	b'zetst
wrong number	Falsche Verbindung	falsh-uh fair-bin-doong

Sightseeing

library	Bibliothek	bib-leo-tek
entrance ticket	Eintrittskarte	ine-tritz-kart-uh
cemetery	Friedhof	freed-hofe
train station	Bahnhof	barn-hofe
gallery	Galerie	gall-er-ree
information	Auskunft	owss-koonft
church	Kirche	keersh-uh
garden	Garten	gart'n
palace/castle	Palast/Schloss	pallast/shloss
place (square)	Platz	plats
bus stop	Haltestelle	hal-te-shtel-uh
national holiday	Nationalfeiertag	nats-yon-ahl-fire-tahk
theatre	Theater	tay-aht-er
free admission	Eintritt frei	ine-tritt fry

Shopping

Do you have/ Is there...?	Gibt es...?	geept ess
How much does it cost?	Was kostet das?	voss kost't duss?
When do you open/ close	Wann öffnen Sie? schliessen Sie?	vunn off'n zee shlees'n zee
this	das	duss
expensive	teuer	toy-er
cheap	preiswert	price-vurt
size	Grösse	gruhs-uh
number	Nummer	noom-er
colour	Farbe	farb-uh
brown	braun	brown
black	schwarz	shvarts
red	rot	roht
blue	blau	blau
green	grün	groon
yellow	gelb	gelp

Types of Shop

antique shop	**Antiquariat**	*antik-var-yat*
chemist (pharmacy)	**Apotheke**	*appo-tay-kuh*
bank	**Bank**	*bunk*
market	**Markt**	*markt*
travel agency	**Reisebüro**	*rye-zer-boo-roe*
department store	**Warenhaus**	*vahr'n-hows*
chemist's drugstore	**Drogerie**	*droog-er-ree*
hairdresser	**Friseur**	*freezz-er*
newspaper kiosk	**Zeitungskiosk**	*tsytoongs-kee-osk*
bookshop	**Buchhandlung**	*bookh-hant-loong*
bakery	**Bäckerei**	*beck-er-eye*
post office	**Post**	*posst*
shop/store	**Geschäft/Laden**	*gush-eft/lard'n*
film processing shop	**Photogeschäft**	*fo-to-gush-eft*
self-service shop	**Selbstbedie-nungsladen**	*selpst-bed-ee-nungs-lard'n*
shoe shop	**Schuhladen**	*shoo-lard'n*
clothes shop store	**Kleiderladen**	*klyder-lard'n*
	Boutique	*boo-teek-uh*
food shop	**Lebensmittel-geschäft**	*lay-bens-mittel-gush-eft*
glass, porcelain	**Glas, Porzellan**	*glars, Port-sellahn*

Staying in a Hotel

Do you have any vacancies?	**Haben Sie noch Zimmer frei?**	*harb'n zee nokh tsimm-er-fry*
with twin beds?	**mit zwei Betten?**	*mitt tsvy bett'n*
with a double bed?	**mit einem Doppelbett?**	*mitt ine'm dopp'lbet*
with a bath?	**mit Bad?**	*mitt bart*
with a shower?	**mit Dusche?**	*mitt doosh-uh*
I have a reservation	**Ich habe eine Reservierung**	*ish harb-uh ine-uh rez-er-veer-oong*
key	**Schlüssel**	*shlooss'l*
porter	**Pförtner**	*pfert-ner*

Eating Out

Do you have a table for …?	**Haben Sie einen Tisch für…?**	*harb'n zee ine-uhn Tisch für…?*
I would like to reserve a table	**Ich möchte eine Reservierung machen**	*ish mer-shtuh ine-uh rezer-veer-oong makh'n*
I'm a vegetarian	**Ich bin Vegetarier**	*ish bin vegg-er-tah-ree-er*
Waiter!	**Herr Ober!**	*hair oh-bare!*
The bill (check), please	**Die Rechnung, bitte**	*dee resh-noong bitt-uh*
breakfast	**Frühstück**	*froo-shtock*
lunch	**Mittagessen**	*mit-targ-ess'n*
dinner	**Abendessen**	*arb'nt-ess'n*
bottle	**Flasche**	*flush-uh*
dish of the day	**Tagesgericht**	*tahg-es-gur-isht*
main dish	**Hauptgericht**	*howpt-gur-isht*
dessert	**Nachtisch**	*nahkh-tish*
cup	**Tasse**	*tass-uh*
wine list	**Weinkarte**	*vine-kart-uh*
tankard	**Krug**	*khroog*
glass	**Glas**	*glars*
spoon	**Löffel**	*lerff'l*
teaspoon	**Teelöffel**	*tay-lerff'l*
tip	**Trinkgeld**	*trink-gelt*

knife	**Messer**	*mess-er*
starter (appetizer)	**Vorspeise**	*for-shpize-uh*
the bill	**Rechnung**	*resh-noong*
plate	**Teller**	*tell-er*
fork	**Gabel**	*gahb'l*

Menu Decoder

Aal	*arl*	eel
Apfel	*upf'l*	apple
Apfelschorle	*upf'l-shoorl-uh*	apple juice with sparkling mineral water
Apfelsine	*upf'l-seen-uh*	orange
Aprikose	*upri-kawz-uh*	apricot
Artischocke	*arti-shokh-uh –*	artichoke
Aubergine	*or-ber-jeen-uh*	aubergine (eggplant)
Banane	*bar-narn-uh*	banana
Beefsteack	*beef-stayk*	steak
Bier	*beer*	beer
Bockwurst	*bokh-voorst*	a type of sausage
Bohnensuppe	*burn-en-zoop-uh*	bean soup
Branntwein	*brant-vine*	spirits
Bratkartoffeln	*brat-kar-toff'ln*	fried potatoes
Bratwurst	*brat-voorst*	fried sausage
Brötchen	*bret-tchen*	bread roll
Brot	*brot*	bread
Brühe	*bruh-uh*	broth
Butter	*boot-ter*	butter
Champignon	*shum-pin-yong*	mushroom
Currywurst	*kha-ree-voorst*	sausage with curry sauce
Dill	*dill*	dill
Ei	*eye*	egg
Eis	*ice*	ice/ ice cream
Ente	*ent-uh*	duck
Erdbeeren	*ayrt-beer'n*	strawberries
Fisch	*fish*	fish
Forelle	*for-ell-uh*	trout
Frikadelle	*Frika-dayl-uh*	rissole/ hamburger
Gans	*ganns*	goose
Garnele	*gar-nayl-uh*	prawn/shrimp
gebraten	*g'braat'n*	fried
gegrillt	*g'grilt*	grilled
gekocht	*g'kokht*	boiled
geräuchert	*g'rowk-ert*	smoked
Geflügel	*g'floog'l*	poultry
Gemüse	*g'mooz-uh*	vegetables
Grütze	*grurt-ser*	groats, gruel
Gulasch	*goo-lush*	goulash
Gurke	*goork-uh*	gherkin
Hammelbraten	*hamm'l-braat'n*	roast mutton
Hähnchen	*haynsh'n*	chicken
Hering	*hair-ing*	herring
Himbeeren	*him-beer'n*	raspberries
Honig	*hoe-nikh*	honey
Kaffee	*kaf-fay*	coffee
Kalbfleisch	*kalp-flysh*	veal
Kaninchen	*ka-neensh'n*	rabbit
Karpfen	*karpf'n*	carp
Kartoffelpüree	*kar-toff'l-poor-ay*	mashed potatoes
Käse	*kayz-uh*	cheese
Kaviar	*kar-vee-ar*	caviar
Knoblauch	*k'nob-lowkh*	garlic
Knödel	*k'nerd'l*	noodle
Kohl	*koal*	cabbage
Kopfsalat	*kopf-zal-aat*	lettuce
Krebs	*krayps*	crab
Kuchen	*kookh'n*	cake

Lachs	*lahkhs*	salmon
Leber	*lay-ber*	liver
mariniert	*mari-neert*	marinated
Marmelade	*marmer-lard-uh*	marmalade, jam
Meerrettich	*may-re-tish*	horseradish
Milch	*milsh*	milk
Mineral-	*minn-er-al-*	mineral
wasser	*vuss-er*	water
Möhre	*mer-uh*	carrot
Nuss	*nooss*	nut
Öl	*erl*	oil
Olive	*o-leev-uh*	olive
Petersilie	*payt-er-zee-li-uh*	parsley
Pfeffer	*pfeff-er*	pepper
Pfirsich	*pfir-zish*	peach
Pflaumen	*pflow-men*	plum
Pommes frites	*pomm-fritt*	chips/ French fries
Quark	*kvark*	soft cheese
Radieschen	*ra-deesh'n*	radish
Rinderbraten	*rind-er-brat'n*	joint of beef
Rinderroulade	*rind-er-roo-lard-uh*	beef olive
Rindfleisch	*rint-flysh*	beef
Rippchen	*rip-sh'n*	cured pork rib
Rotkohl	*roht-koal*	red cabbage
Rüben	*rhoob'n*	turnip
Rührei	*rhoo-er-eye*	scrambled eggs
Saft	*zuft*	juice
Salat	*zal-aat*	salad
Salz	*zults*	salt
Salzkartoffeln	*zults-kar-toff'l*	boiled potatoes
Sauerkirschen	*zow-er-keersh'n*	cherries
Sauerkraut	*zow-er-krowt*	sauerkraut
Sekt	*zekt*	sparkling wine
Senf	*zenf*	mustard
scharf	*sharf*	spicy
Schaschlik	*shash-lik*	kebab
Schlagsahne	*shlahgg-zarn-uh*	whipped cream
Schnittlauch	*shnit-lowkh*	chives
Schnitzel	*shnitz'l*	veal or pork cutlet
Schweinefleisch	*shvine-flysh*	pork
Spargel	*shparg'l*	asparagus
Spiegelei	*shpeeg'l-eye*	fried egg
Spinat	*shpin-art*	spinach
Tee	*tay*	tea
Tomate	*tom-art-uh*	tomato
Wassermelone	*vuss-er-me-lohn-uh*	watermelon
Wein	*vine*	wine
Weintrauben	*vine-trowb'n*	grapes
Wiener	*veen-er*	frankfurter
Würstchen	*voorst-sh'n*	
Zander	*tsan-der*	pike-perch
Zitrone	*tsi-trohn-uh*	lemon
Zucker	*tsook-er*	sugar
Zwieback	*tsvee-ba*	rusk
Zwiebel	*tsveeb'l*	onion

Numbers

	German	Pronunciation
0	null	*nool*
1	eins	*eye'ns*
2	zwei	*tsvy*
3	drei	*dry*
4	vier	*feer*
5	fünf	*foonf*
6	sechs	*zex*
7	sieben	*zeeb'n*
8	acht	*uhkht*
9	neun	*noyn*
10	zehn	*tsayn*
11	elf	*elf*
12	zwölf	*tserlf*
13	dreizehn	*dry-tsayn*
14	vierzehn	*feer-tsayn*
15	fünfzehn	*foonf-tsayn*
16	sechzehn	*zex-tsayn*
17	siebzehn	*zeep-tsayn*
18	achtzehn	*uhkht-tsayn*
19	neunzehn	*noyn-tsayn*
20	zwanzig	*tsvunn-tsig*
21	einundzwanzig	*ine-oont-tsvunn-tsig*
30	dreissig	*dry-sig*
40	vierzig	*feer-sig*
50	fünfzig	*foonf-tsig*
60	sechzig	*zex-tsig*
70	siebzig	*zeep-tsig*
80	achtzig	*uhkht-tsig*
90	neunzig	*noyn-tsig*
100	hundert	*hoond't*
1000	tausend	*towz'nt*
1,000,000	eine Million	*ine-uh mill-yon*

Time

	German	Pronunciation
one minute	eine Minute	*ine-uh min-oot-uh*
one hour	eine Stunde	*ine-uh shtoond-uh*
half an hour	eine halbe Stunde	*ine-uh hullb-uh shtoond-uh*
Monday	Montag	*mohn-targ*
Tuesday	Dienstag	*deens-targ*
Wednesday	Mittwoch	*mitt-vokh*
Thursday	Donnerstag	*donn-ers-targ*
Friday	Freitag	*fry-targ*
Saturday	Samstag/	*zums-targ*
	Sonnabend	*zonn-ah-bent*
Sunday	Sonntag	*zon-targ*
January	Januar	*yan-ooar*
February	Februar	*fay-brooar*
March	März	*mairts*
April	April	*april*
May	Mai	*my*
June	Juni	*yoo-ni*
July	Juli	*yoo-lee*
August	August	*ow-goost*
September	September	*zep-tem-ber*
October	Oktober	*ok-toh-ber*
November	November	*no-vem-ber*
December	Dezember	*day-tsem-ber*
spring	Frühling	*froo-ling*
summer	Sommer	*zomm-er*
autumn (fall)	Herbst	*hairpst*
winter	Winter	*vint-er*

ACKNOWLEDGMENTS

This edition updated by

Contributors Petra Falkenberg, Gabby Innes, Alexander Rennie

Senior Editors Alison McGill, Zoë Rutland

Senior Designers Laura O'Brien, Vinita Venugopal, Ira Sharma

Editors Ilina Choudhary, Lucy Sara-Kelly

Assistant Art Editor Mrunali Sanjay Likhar

Proofreader Debra Wolter

Indexer Helen Peters

Picture Researcher Manager Taiyaba Khatoon

Senior Picture Researcher Nishwan Rasool

Assistant Picture Research Administrator Manpreet Kaur

Publishing Assistant Simona Velikova

Jacket Designer Laura O'Brien

Jacket Picture Researcher Laura Richardson

Cartography Simonetta Giori

Senior Cartographic Editor James MacDonald

Cartography Manager Suresh Kumar

Senior DTP Designer Tanveer Zaidi

DTP Designers Rohit Rojal, Ashok Kumar, Syed Md Farhan

Pre-production Manager Balwant Singh

Image Retouching-Production Manager Pankaj Sharma

Senior Production Controller Samantha Cross

Managing Editors Shikha Kulkarni, Beverly Smart, Hollie Teague

Managing Art Editors Gemma Doyle

Senior Managing Art Editor Priyanka Thakur

Art Director Maxine Pedliham

Publishing Director Georgina Dee

DK would like to thank the following for their contribution to the previous editions: Petra Falkenberg, Anna Streiffert

The publisher would like to thank the following for their kind permission to reproduce their photographs:

Key: a-above; b-below/bottom; c-centre; f-far; l-left; r-right; t-top

123RF.com: fritzundkatze 153br, jarino47 51t, stavrida 84.

Alamy Stock Photo: © Adam Eastland 156, Agencja Fotograficzna Caro / Christoph Eckelt 107, Agencja Fotograficzna Caro / Muhs 121, Agencja Fotograficzna Caro / Ponizak 139, Agencja Fotograficzna Caro / Schwarz 26cla, Agencja Fotograficzna Caro / Sorge 31tr, Art Kowalsky 97, Bildagentur-online 33cr, Bildagentur-online / Joko 39tr, Bildagentur-online / Joko 94, Bildagentur-online / McPhoto 44b, Bildagentur-online / Schoening 99, Bildagentur-online / Schoening 124, Bildagentur-online / Schoening 142, Eden Breitz 105t, Eden Breitz 105b, Eden Breitz 106t, Jo Chambers 39cra, charistoone-images 60b, CMA / BOT 28b, Ian G Dagnall 85, Peter Delius 34-35t, dpa picture alliance 154–155b, edpics 70b, edpics 71b, Oscar Elias 34b, EPX 23br, FALKENSTEINFOTO 9tl, Folio Images 38, Eddy Galeotti 12br, Angela Serena Gilmour 40, Angela Serena Gilmour 47b, Andrew Hasson 13cl, Borgese Maurizio / Hemis.fr 120t, Hauser Patrice / Hemis.fr 129, Maisant Ludovic / Hemis fr 13tl, Serrano Anna / Hemis.fr 63b, Juergen Henkelmann 37b, Juergen Henkelmann 39cla, Historic Images 9cr, Peter Horree 106b, IanDagnall Computing 10cl, Image Professional GmbH / travelstock44 25br, Imagebroker / Arco / Schoening 13clb (9), Imagebroker / Arco / Schoening Berlin 17, imageBROKER / Henning Hattendorf 95tl, imageBROKER / Karl-Heinz Spremberg 104, imageBROKER / Schoening 119tl, imageBROKER / Schoening 157, imageBROKER / Schoening Berlin 79b, imageBROKER com GmbH & Co. KG / Norbert Michalke 11, imageBROKER.com GmbH & Co. KG / Peter Schickert 143tl, Imago 125b, INTERFOTO / Personalities 45, Joko 103b, Jon Arnold Images Ltd / Michele Falzone 53, Albert Knapp 56t, Lebrecht Music & Arts 10br, Iain Masterton 35b, Iain Masterton 46b, Iain Masterton 47t, Iain Masterton 56b, Iain Masterton 136, Iain Masterton 149b, mauritius images GmbH / Rer Mattes 27t, Niday Picture Library 8, Cum Okolo 13cla, Werner Otto 41b, Panther Media GmbH / Joerg Hackemann / meinzahn 63t, peter. forsberg 69t, Pictorial Press 32b, Pictorial Press 64t, Pictorial Press 65, Pictorial Press Ltd 10tl, PjrArt 127b, robertharding / Frank Fell 13bl, robertharding / Frank Fell 66, S.Popovic RM 98, Joern Sackermann 25t, Schoening 114, Schoening 128, Michael Kuenne / PRESSCOV / Sipa USA 30b, Dave Stamboulis 101, Marek Stepan 102, travelstock44.de / Juergen Held 68, travelstock44.de / Juergen Held 83b, travelstock44.de / Juergen Held 113t ravelstock44.de / Juergen Held 151, Urbanmyth 2cr, UtCon Collection 9tr.

Ankerklause: Wolfgang Borrs 138t.

AWL Images: Sabine Lubenow 6–7.

Berlinale: Andreas Teich 86.

Berliner Kaffeerösterei: 130.

Depositphotos Inc: Patryk_Kosmider 91, maxsol7 81b.

Deutsche Kinemathek: Hans Scherhaufer 32t.

Deutsche Oper: Marcus Lieberenz 72.

Dreamstime.com: 54, AGfoto 81t, Belusuab 94t, Cbechinie 115, Ccat82 117t, Claudiodivizia 49cr, Danielal 13clb, Danielal 144b, Davidstiller 81cb, Dennis Dolkens 21br, Draghicich 153t, Elenaburn 110t, Elxeneize 10bl, Elxeneize 89, Erix2005 162, Santiago Rodríguez Fontoba 59b, Giuseppemasci 58, Diego Grandi 16tl, Diego Grandi 42br, Diego Grandi 43b, Gunold 113b, Hanohiki 57b, Hel080808 93b, Javarman 111b, Josefkubes 141b, Junede 126-127t, Konrad Kerker 123t, Sergey Kohl 87, Anna Krivitskaia 87tl, Madrabothair 23bl, Vasilii Maslak 14cb (Philharmonie), Mateuszolszowy 49b, Aliaksandr Mazurkevich 70t, Mistervlad 160, Mistervlad 161b, Jaroslav Moravcik 14bc, Luciano Mortula 65t, Luciano Mortula 133t, Luciano Mortula 147t, Peter Moulton 27b, NGSpacetime 110b, Sergiy Palamarchuk 12cra, Anna Para 37cl, Jean Pavone 159t, Pundapanda 67, Roberto Rizzi 80, Rudi1976 60t, Sergiomonti 23cb, Sylvaindeutsch 62t, Tomas1111 92, Val_th 41t, VanderWolfImages 16ca, Hilda Weges 109t, Sylvia Wendorf 144t, Kim Willems 26b, Virestock 20cla, Noppasin Wongchum 12crb, Yorgy67 44t, Alex Zarubin 118.

Getty Images: AFP / - / Stringer 64b, Corbis Documentary / Maremagnum 30t, Sean Gallup Staff 28t, Hulton Archive / Estate of Emil Bieber / Klaus Niermann 9br, Hulton Fine Art Collection / Fine Art Images / Heritage Images 48b, Hulton Fine Art Collection / Heritage Images 29, Moment / RICOWde 33b, The Image Bank / Grant Faint 165, Schöning / Ullstein bild 154t, Westend61 148–149t.

Getty Images / iStock: Andrey Danilovich 83t, E+ / mbbirdy 19, E+ / Nikada 5, Heiko119 16crb, holgs 20br, ka_ru 120b, Nikada 21clb, Noppasin 14cb, Leonardo Patrizi 22, Robert Wygoda 21ca.

Gugelhof: 145.

Restaurant & Café Heider: 163.

HoW: 76.

Jewish Museum Berlin: Spertus Institute Chicago / Roman März 51br, Yves Sucksdorff 50–51b.

Klunkerkranich: Julian Nelken 138b.

Matrix: 150.

Mein Haus am See: 77t.

Overkill GmbH: 137.

Restaurant Lubitsch Berlin: 131.

Robert Harding Picture Library: Ingo Schulz 41t.

Schwules Museum: Tobias Wille 75.

Shutterstock.com: Alizada Studios 36, KievVictor 96, LuisPinaPhotography 112, Grzegorz_Pakula 42–43t, Ugis Riba 24–25b, Manfred Roeben 134, Scharfsinn 16cla, Noppasin Wongchum 15.

Victoria Bar: 79t.

Sheet Map Cover Image:
Unsplash: Florian Wehde.

Cover Images:
Front and Spine: **Unsplash**: Florian Wehde.
Back: **Alamy Stock Photo:** robertharding / Frank Fell tl; **Getty Images / iStock:** E+ / mbbirdy cl, Leonardo Patrizi tr.

All other images © Dorling Kindersley Limited
For further information see: www.dkimages.com

First edition 2002

Published in Great Britain by
Dorling Kindersley Limited,
DK, One Embassy Gardens, 8 Viaduct
Gardens, London SW11 7BW, UK

The authorised representative in the EEA is
Dorling Kindersley Verlag GmbH. Arnulfstr.
124, 80636 Munich, Germany

Published in the United States by
DK Publishing, 1745 Broadway, 20th Floor,
New York, NY 10019, USA

Copyright © 2002, 2024 Dorling
Kindersley Limited
A Penguin Random House Company

24 25 26 27 10 9 8 7 6 5 4 3 2 1

The publishers cannot accept responsibility for any consequences
arising from the use of this book, nor for any material on third party
websites, and cannot guarantee that any website address in this
book will be a suitable source of travel information.

A CIP catalog record is available
from the British Library.

A catalog record for this book is available
from the Library of Congress.

ISSN: 1479-344X

ISBN: 978-0-2416-7624-0

Printed and bound in China

www.dk.com

This book was made with Forest
Stewardship Council™ certified
paper – one small step in DK's
commitment to a sustainable future.
Learn more at **www.dk.com/uk/
information/sustainability**